Battling Bentleys in Belgium

BENTLEY RECORD BREAKING

AT ANTWERP and GHENT

1959 to 1976

Johnnie Winther

The W.O. Bentley Memorial Foundation
Publication Number 5

ISBN 978-0-9540901-4-2

Designed and printed in England by

Quorum Print Services Ltd.
Unit 3 & 4 Lansdown Industrial Estate
Gloucester Road
Cheltenham
Gloucestershire
GL51 8PL
01242 584984

For the publishers

The W.O. Bentley Memorial Foundation
Ironstone Lane
Wroxton
Banbury
Oxfordshire
OX15 6ED

Index

Dedication   4

Introduction   5

Acknowledgements   7

The Beginning   9

The Preparations   11

Arrival in Belgium   15

Final Preparations   24

Trackside at the Trials   33

Forrest Lycett in 1959   44

Jumbo Jet in 1972   48

Conclusions   52

Appendix 1   Antwerp Results   1959 to 1965   57

Appendix 2   Ghent Results   1967 to 1976   63

Appendix 3   Fastest Bentley Performance each Year 1959 – 1976   74

Appendix 4   Drivers and their Bentleys achieving runs of over   75
              100 mph in order of speed

Appendix 5   Drivers who competed in a Bentley in the Trials in   81
              alphabetical order

Tailpiece   Belgian Recollections   83

This little volume is dedicated to the late John Nutter, revered 'Headmaster' of the Archivists and formerly Chairman of the Trustees of the W O Memorial Foundation.

I couple John's name with that of W O Bentley, who John so admired and who of course made the Speed Trials possible by designing and building the Bentleys of the 1920s and early 1930s that competed.

I feel we should not omit mention of those who breathed on the Bentleys involved to squeeze yet greater performance from them.

Finally I record my deepest respect and admiration for the numerous members of the Bentley Drivers Club who intrepidly drove with such verve at both Antwerp and Ghent in the years from 1959 to 1976.

John Nutter at Antwerp in 1965

John Nutter at Speed competing in his Bentley 6½ at Antwerp.

4

Introduction

This little monograph is the result of a proposal by the late John Nutter, distinguished long term member of the Bentley Drivers Club and Trustee of the W O Bentley Memorial Foundation, wherein he was affectionately known to that body's archivists as "the Headmaster". A cunningly worded series of letters from him finally trapped one of his pupil archivists, who had been hoping to evade his eagle eye, and asked whether the writer would be prepared to try and put on record the Speed Trials that Bentleys took part in first at Antwerp and then subsequently at Ghent in Belgium between 1959 and 1976 when astonishing results were achieved.

Recording the results has been a comparatively simple task, thanks to the heroic efforts of fellow archivist Derek Ayres, who dug out from copies of the BDC Reviews of the period all the reports written following each year's Trial. The writer was given these by the Headmaster as "homework to keep you out of the pub" to read, mark, learn and inwardly digest with the objective of producing a work to attempt to encapsulate the background, atmosphere of the Trials each year, and to honour those who took part and achieved so much. It has been a privilege to have been selected to carry out this task. Whether I have succeeded I leave to you who reads what follows to judge. All I can say is that it has given me immense pleasure in compiling the contents. I am, of course, greatly indebted to those members of the BDC who wrote up each Trial each year for the Review from whom I frequently quote verbatim. Their names are listed for reference under Acknowledgements.

We also appealed in both the Foundation Corner section of the BDC Review of October 2009 for photographs of Bentleys that took part and of the Trials themselves to supplement the pictorial collection held in the Archives at Wroxton. Following this I then wrote to each traceable surviving BDC member who participated in the Trials, asking for their own personal reminiscences of these now somewhat distant events. I am extremely grateful to those who responded and their comments are included in the relevant text or after the summary of the applicable Trial's results listed in Appendix 1 & 2. Without the help of these members this little work would merely have been in a position to list statistics and bald facts and not describe, as I have attempted to do, the elements of camaraderie, cooperation, and dedication of the participants themselves that pervaded the Trials. It goes without stating the obvious that without the efforts of those members who took part in the Trials there would be no story to relate at all.

This text has also been greatly enlivened by the inclusion of excerpts from conversations at a gathering early in 2010 at the home of Dick and Ann Moss which were recorded by the indefatigable Alan Bodfish from the Archive Department of the Foundation at Wroxton. Those present who participated included Edward Barraclough, Harvey Hine, David Llewellyn, Peter Morley, Dick Moss, Tom Rose and Martin Trentham – their reminiscences and anecdotes add much to the contents of this work, in adding colour and bringing to life the atmosphere that pervaded at the Speed Trials in those decades of yore. I owe much to them for the time they gave to contribute to this little volume and I know those reading it will be equally appreciative of their recollections.

Finally may I apologise in advance for any errors or omissions that have crept into the facts contained herein, particularly in the Appendices where I suspect, due to my lack of diligence, misplacement of decimal points will have occurred in more than one figure!

Acknowledgements

PAST BENTLEY DRIVERS CLUB MEMBERS WHO HAVE CONTRIBUTED TO THIS PUBLICATION

Their works I have pilfered shamelessly and quoted frequently in attempts to bring the narrative alive. It is largely due to their reports in BDC Reviews that we can have a picture of each Trial.

Jack Bailey	De Trek Naar Antwerpen 1963	BDC Review	July 1963
	Gandering in Gand	" "	July 1967
	A Most Enjoyable Ghent	" "	July 1969
	Bentleys in Action	" "	October 1970
Bill Cheston	The Battle of Crewe	BDC Review	1973
	Ghent 1974	" "	1974
Peter Corney	Report of 1959 Trial	BDC Review	September 1959
	Day of Belgian Records	" "	July 1962
	Ghent 1968	" "	July 1968
Barry Eastick	Dag der Belgische Rekords Antwerpen	BDC Review	July 1964
	Ghent 1975	" "	1975
Forrest Lycett	My Own Part in a Vintage Bentley Party at Herendals Antwerp 1959		
Gordon Russell	10th Anniversary of Ghent	BDC Review	1976
Geoffrey Sandwith	Antwerp 9th May 1965	BDC Review	July 1965
Stanley Sedgwick	Mainly about Bentleys Motoring My Way		
Mike Wilcock	Ghent 1974	BDC Review	1976

Acknowledgements - continued

PRESENT BENTLEY DRIVERS CLUB MEMBERS WHO HAVE CONTRIBUTED TO THIS PUBLICATION.

By their reminiscences of their time at the Speed Trials which add great colour to the describing of these events.

Don Balmer, Edward Barraclough, Harvey Hine, David Llewellyn, Peter Morley, Dick and Ann Moss, John Proctor, Philip and Vicky Sandwith, Martin Trentham.

I am very grateful to each of them for their valuable contributions and I apologise if I have inadvertently omitted anybody.

Finally but far from least I must record in spite of his modesty the enormous debt I owe to Alan Bodfish, WO Bentley Memorial Foundation Administrator at Wroxton. Alan patiently unearthed and incorporated the photographs which enliven the text as well as expertly interviewing those mentioned above to reveal their recollections of the events they took part in now over a third of a century ago.

The Beginning

It seems that like so much in the early post World War Two History of the Bentley Drivers Club, the concept of engaging in Speed Trials in Belgium originated in the fertile brain of Stanley Sedgwick. In his book "Motoring My Way" he writes "The idea entered my head sometime before Christmas (1958) that it might be possible to arrange for the well known Jabbeke Aeltre stretch of the Ostend Brussels autoroute to be closed for the purpose of timed runs over a measured kilometre and a measured mile. The object of the venture in Belgium was for each participant to cover a measured mile and kilometre in both directions from both standing and flying starts on the motor road, closed to the public for the duration of the Trials."

Can we conceive, in these days of over officious "Elf n' Sayftee" risk aversion and mountainous E U Regulations, such an occurrence today? John Nutter told me "Quite what politics went on behind the scenes in Belgium enabling motorways to be closed; I don't think we ever fully understood. We were told

The President musing at Antwerp in 1959

that these closures were obtained only because the regular attendance of the mad English in their funny old cars was somehow made out to be of benefit to the Belgian Tourist Industry." Whatever the justification, motorways were closed for such events in the 1950s in Belgium. Forrest Lycett had been at Jabbeke in 1950 when at the wheel of his famous 8 litre Bentley he had set up new Belgian National Class 'B' Records for the flying kilometre and flying mile at 134.755 mph and 133.828 mph respectively.

I suspect one of Stanley Sedgwick's motives in dreaming of a further Speed Trial on the Jabbeke-Aeltre stretch of the Belgian autoroute was to see whether Forrest Lycett could once more raise the 8 litre's speed to regain the records he had achieved back in 1950. Lycett did agree to join in and this, in his own words "was solely due to the benevolent yet persistent importunity of Stanley Sedgwick, President of the Bentley Drivers Club and its good Shepherd, for truth to tell I had been but lukewarm at best."

Sedgwick himself writes in "Motoring My Way" "We were anxious to see the 8 litre take back the honours from Maurice Trintignant of France, who had improved on the 8 litre's 1950 speeds in a Facel Vega reaching 139.895 mph and 140.186 mph for the kilometre and mile respectively." So thanks to Stanley the idea developed subsequently.

The Preparations

Once Stanley Sedgwick had persuaded Forrest Lycett to participate, it became a matter of turning the dream into reality. Permission to close the autoroute was sought from the Belgian Government through the Royal Automobile Club of Belgium to carry out the tests. The Belgian Government alas refused, not surprisingly, due to the heavy daily usage of this stretch of the road between the coast at Ostend and the capital of Brussels. However, they countered agreeably by offering part of a new motor road in course of construction between Antwerp and Liege, a brand new concrete road surface of a length of about ten kilometres.

"The regulations for such Speed Trial record attempts require the distance to be covered in both directions within an hour, and it must be the same piece of road" as Stanley Sedgwick related in his work "Mainly about Bentleys" – "when a mile and kilometre are being timed it is usual to measure off the mile and place the kilometre at one end of and within the mile. Flying runs can thus be timed over both the mile and kilometre on a single run; this is so in both directions. There are strict limitations as to permitted gradients at each end of the measured distances which themselves have to be level with very small tolerances." At the offered stretch near the village of Herrentals "there was a 3 kilometres run-in at one end of the measured mile and 5 kilometres at the other". This gave plenty of distance for participants to wind up their Bentleys to maximum speed before entering the timed distances and, equally important, ample distance for slowing down after completing the measured mile! It is interesting to note that the M1 motorway in England has no stretch that can comply with these requirements.

Stanley Sedgwick next turned the meticulous administrative side of his brain to the preparations for the event itself. A torrent of paperwork in early May engulfed those members who had signed up following an announcement in Bentley Drivers Club Notes. Peter Corney wrote in 1959 "sheets fully describing every detailed move and proposal from Dover back to Dover including arrangements for hotel accommodation, shipping, personnel list, spares list in English and French, details of petrol and oil facilities, tyres – in fact the lot". All sent out by post to each participant by the painstaking Stanley Sedgwick. John Goddard in 1962 wrote "very soon the gen sheets began to circulate – the President was busy again: information about tyres facilities, hotel accommodation including leaflets brochures and prices, cross-channel transport and suggested alternatives to suit all tastes and geographical locations, vaccination certificates, petrol and oil facilities, regulations, entry forms, competition numbers, questionnaires concerning competing cars for the information of the Belgian press, lists of competitors, spectators, street maps of Antwerp, details of who was travelling which way and on what day were all crammed into these digests". This shows the scope of the task of preparatory organisation undertaken by Stanley Sedgwick. As a side note by John Goddard in 1962 stated "very early on in the proceedings (for that year) Stan announced he would not be shouldering the enormous burden of organising the whole project as he had done in 1959 – as far as one could see the only difference was the necessity of individuals to make their own arrangements for crossing the channel, instead of as in 1959 being booked in the main as a party!" John Goddard added in 1962 "Stan's announcement must have been the understatement of the year!"

In later years the task of producing "the gen" for participants fell on other shoulders – notably those of 'Rusty' Russ Turner particularly for the Trials at Ghent.

The Belgians had a quaint custom of asking competitors to fill in their nicknames on the entry forms. They then used this name in the programmes and on all official timing lists. The BDC Reviews of the time lists a number

Rusty Russ-Turner – Organiser of BDC participation in the Trials after Stanley Sedgwick, seated in the ex Birkin Supercharged 4½ Litre.

12

of these – "Club Chauffeur" as Harvey Hine described himself. Dick Tindell masqueraded under the soubriquet of "Lemonade" for some reason. "Uncle Pipe" was no less than John Nutter, called this apparently by youngsters due to the implement he smoked in those days! The Review also mentions a "Monsieur Bespoke" and a "Monsieur Poofter" – but thankfully not their real identities.

Peter Morley comments also: "One of my nick-names was to do with the milk churn and people think I used to use milk churns to put under the loading plates of the Napier, but really it was a one gallon milk churn which I took around when I went to buy Bentleys, always with notes in it and that is the actual true story, it's the pound notes, not the scotches under the planks!"

Harvey Hine fondly recalls: "Fred Hofmann used to come to Belgium and he used to bring that lovely guy Jerry Stolger who owned the hotel at Dorchester on Thames – chap with the motorbikes and his mate "Moley". Anyway this guy – not at Dorchester now, he used to come with Fred Hofmann and they used to get up to all sorts of mischief – didn't they? They were all having dinner one night at Dorchester on Thames and Jerry who owned the place suddenly turned up in the dining room with his 1100 cc Kawasaki riding it around the dining room. Jerry always had the most beautiful girls as waitresses at his establishment."

For the initial visit to Antwerp a one ton diesel van was provided by David Llewellyn and fully loaded with spares, tools and tyres at Henley on Thames by Fred Hoffman. This was then driven to Dover and onto the ferry to add support to the venture at Antwerp. A lengthy journey as Peter Corney describes: "For the van I have the greatest admiration, being in all respects a very tractable and manoeuvrable vehicle and gear changing was a pleasure (provided you imagined you had a B box and no clutch stop)!" Corney mentions the van having less than half the speed of the slowest Bentley. It took from landing at Ostend at 4.30 pm until 9.45 pm before Antwerp was reached. It must have been a tedious trip which culminated in Fred Hoffman picking out a pedestrian on the outskirts for Peter Corney to ask the way using his best French, only to be directed in one of the broadest Scottish accents he'd heard in years! The two intrepid van men encountered an hour and a half wait on the return journey at the Belgian/French frontier where the customs discovered one more tyre than the number listed on the documentation.

Peter Morley recalls his encounter with Customs: "We took the Sunbeam Napier over there with Gordon Russell. We obviously did not have a log book so they said you must be exporting the car. We said "no, we are racing it over there". They said "people don't race cars like this" and they kept us on the quayside for 24 hours. Gordon and I did not have hardly anything to eat or drink, so in the end we had to pay £700 deposit before they would let us go.

Gordon gave them a cheque and as soon as we drove off he rang Avril (my wife) and she cancelled the cheque so they weren't gong to get any money anyway".

Peter Morley also relates: "coming back and being a non smoker I didn't bother to bring any cigars back so when I got to the Customs they said "Anything to Declare?". I said "No", but unbeknown to me when I got to the other side Jack Bailey had filled up my Pacey-Hassan with boxes of cigars! That's the sort of tricks you had to contend with those chaps."

Harvey Hine remembers Jack Bailey outwitting the Customs: "Talking about jerry cans, Jack Bailey, he had a special water can he took it through the Customs; he filled it up with whisky and on return had it in the back of his car all perfectly open and pretended it was petrol."

Dick Moss recalls returning from Ghent: "I met Ian Weston in his 4½ and we came back together to get the ferry at Ostend. We arrived there late in the evening and I said I am going to see if we can get some covered storage for my car and would you like to join me? He said he would. So I went to the nearest garage and said: "I have got two old cars, is there any chance we can park them up in your garage for the night?" And he said "absolutely no way" but he added "what sort of cars are they?" So I said "they are Vintage Bentleys". He said "give me half an hour and I will have the place cleared." Half an hour later his showroom was empty. We parked both of the cars in the showroom and I went back in about an hour and the cars were very nicely shown on display. There's a table and a plate and wine bottles and glasses and he's charging people to come in to have a look at the cars!!"

It can be said some good has come from the European Union in that at least we no longer have to face the hassle of customs inspections while travelling within it over on the continent.

Arrival In Belgium

The ferry route chosen from Dover varied from year to year – sometimes to Ostend, other occasions to Zeebrugge, even by Hovercraft to Calais. Jack Bailey commented drily on the 1967 voyage: "It was rather trying in that it needed both hands on when trying to walk, making the carrying of glasses and bottles somewhat difficult" – other crossings were happily smoother.

Edward Barraclough relates: "I went to Antwerp in 1963 with my father in law, Frank Sowden, with his 8 litre. It was really just a party which started going across on the boat at Dover or wherever it was going to cross to Ostend. I think Peter Corney used to buy a full bottle of Drambuie and drink it before we got to Ostend; we helped him a little as well!"

Perhaps the following conversation in 2010 indicates the atmosphere en route off the track: "A lot of people came, although they didn't have cars, they came for the party, hangers-on and riding mechanics." Alan Bodfish: "So they were as much social events as driving events?" Edward Barraclough; "Very much so, very few ladies there." Peter Morley; "A few women but not many ladies!"

In 1972 the crossing was by Hovercraft. The party were marshalled aboard by an exceedingly pretty hostess who was asked by a Bentley driver, whose name is not divulged, if she still had skirt trouble! The hostess took some persuading that the enquiry was directed at the rubber Hovercraft skirt and not the delightfully brief mini she was sporting. – Indeed?!

Tom Rose recollects a difficult time he experienced crossing the Channel: "In those days on ferry boats you drove down one side to a sort of turntable at the end that pushed the car round and you drove back down the other side of the boat to get off. I got to the turntable sitting in the car and a great big seaman came along and started pushing on the wing. I was trying to get him not to push on the bodywork but to push on the wheel and he didn't really understand. Neil Corner appeared and told the seaman to push on the wheel, the seaman turned round and said in English "I'm not bloody well paid to push wheels, I push bodies". I was stuck in the car and couldn't open the door so Neil summoned the deck officer who appeared and supported the seaman. So Neil pushed the car round on the turntable for me and then we formed up in front of Stanley Sedgwick saying "look, you know this really isn't good enough". Stanley got hold of the captain of the ship and these two blokes were thrown off, and left on the quay at Ostend! I remember that terribly well."

In 1969 Mike Wilcock had an interesting crossing with his 8 litre on a cargo

Geoffrey Sandwith loading his 4½ to fly across to Antwerp in 1962.

boat from Jersey which, on arrival at that island, had a full load of cornflakes. On docking it was raining and the cornflakes could not be unloaded in case the flakes got wet! As a result Mike had to hang around from the Tuesday when he had expected to sail until Thursday; however he arrived safely on time in Ghent.

Martin Trentham relates: "I came to the Speed Trials fairly late because, although I had a 4½, I decided to build a Mark VI Special. In 1975 the car was still in the process of being built but my parents and I were due for a holiday in the South of France so we called in at Ghent just to see what was going on and that was obviously our first taste of it. The following year the car (Mark VI Special) was ready although it was rather a last minute thing because the main Bentley party were going over on the Thursday prior to the weekend, I was actually having my MoT test on the Thursday, which was the first MoT the car had ever had as a Special. Of course it was completely newly built so it had no miles on the clock. So having got the MoT I drove the 10 miles down to the Warwick by-pass, and I drove up and down the by-pass for several hours and clocked up 300 miles and returned home to go to bed. I got up early the next morning to catch the ferry at 11.35 from Dover. I went down in convoy with another Mark VI (Charles Teall) and we drove all the way down on Friday morning having unfortunately missed the Bentley party on the Thursday evening. Of course in those days it was the North Circular road instead of the M25 and I had overheating problems but we managed to get over there alright."

Peter Morley remembers with sadness: "On the ferry having my jerry cans of fuel pinched, new jerry cans for the occasion and full and when I got to the other side, there weren't any cans on the lorry. So nothing is new is it?"

In 1959 on arrival at Ostend and passed through customs inspection the cars were lined up and various tanks drained of their "Golden Esso" which was then unobtainable in Belgium and therefore to be reserved for Forrest Lycett's 8 litre which pinked badly on petrols of lower octane values.

At this point it seems appropriate to record the generous sponsorship the ventures received each year from various sources. In 1959 Esso made petrol and oil available free of charge both for travelling and for the speed tests. In 1962 Shell Mex and BP generously took over the free supply of fuel and oil at Antwerp and put the services of Jean Lahaye, BP's racing manager in Belgium, at the BDC participants' disposal. In 1968 it was Castrol who made a substantial amount of oil free to each Bentley competitor and Messrs Link Hampson Ltd provided a free supply of STP together with overalls – very welcome during that time of squeeze, freeze on prices and incomes. In the final year of the Ghent Trials in 1976 Pace Petroleum sponsored the Club's attendance and also gave a party for the Bentley team and the Committee Sportif of the RAC des Flandres. It goes without saying these various companies offered much appreciated support which greatly helped to alleviate the financial burden of the venture on those competing, and the BDC responded and amply demonstrated its gratitude for this with numerous commemorative presentational awards to the generous donors.

Dunlops feature strongly in the support they gave. In 1959 participants were instructed to send their tyres to Dunlop for inspection; an order for any new racing tyres and tubes required had been placed and the tyres were to be buffed by Dunlop according to the estimated maximum speeds to be attained. Dunlops also suggested where possible wheels to be used should be sent to them for covers to be fitted. They also provided the full time services of D J MacDonald (the legendary "Dunlop Mac") to accompany the participants from start to finish, who were naturally greatly indebted to that organisation for their comprehensive advice to the venture in both its first year 1959 and subsequently.

Harvey Hine concurs: "Well I was invited to go on this trip by Rusty (Russ Turner) and the temptation was that Dunlops were going to give us 50% off the cost of racing tyres and that was a huge bonus."

Support in other highly pertinent ways came from various organisations

En route to Antwerp in 1965.

and individuals on arrival in Belgium. Particular mention must be made of the Antwerp Motor Union. Whereas in 1959 the concept of the first visit to Belgium had, as we have seen, been the brain child of Stanley Sedgwick, the next visit came about as a direct result of a formal invitation by the Antwerp Motor Union to take part in their official Day of Belgian National Records. In 1962 the AMU arranged the hotel bookings for the Bentley participants at a strategically placed and suitable location – the Antwerp Docks Hotel.

Harvey Hine remembers the Bentleyists at this hotel: "Stanley (Sedgwick) was trying to keep us under control but in the hotel there was quite a lot of transiting over the roof; people climbing out of bedroom windows across the roofs of the hotel and going into other bedroom windows to escape from Stan". Sedgwick was a teetotaller and strongly disapproved of his flock imbibing before the Trials on the morrow insisting they should be safely tucked up in bed early in the evening.

The AMU also arranged transport for the Bentley party to and from various functions. In 1962 their President, Maurice Rosen, and their Club Secretary, Tony Stappaerts, greeted the Bentleyists at the Brasserie Race Flag – being the first of many offers of hospitality enjoyed that year. What subsequently amazed the Bentley party was that at that time the AMU comprised a mere 30 members! As Peter Corney wrote in the BDC Review of July 1962 "There are no words to illustrate adequately the sincere goodwill, hospitality and unstinted generosity which the Antwerp Motor Union members went out of their way to provide. Nothing was too much trouble to them in their extremely successful effort to ensure that everyone in the BDC was made more than welcome."

c.c. Lt. Col. Berthon
    Mr. Kramer
    Mr. Russ-Turner

Greensleeves,
Leigh Place,
Cobham, Surrey.   13th May, 1964

Mr. A. Stappaerts,
Antwerp Motor Union,
Ontropstraat 3,
Antwerp,
Belgium.

        Now that dust has settled a little after my return, I write to you on behalf of my Committee to put on record our sincere appreciation of the magnificent trophy which you have presented to this Club.

        It really is a most generous act and we would all like you to make it known to your Members that their generosity is appreciated and the trophy will always be held in high esteem.

        As you know, we decided that so long as there is a Flying Kilometre at Antwerp, it will be awarded to the Member putting up the best performance in a Bentley.   This year it has been awarded to Frank Sowden and I can tell you that he is very proud of it.

        I do hope that you will be visiting England again sometime soon and it is to be hoped that such a visit would coincide with an important meeting of our Club so that you could meet old faces free from the responsibilities of organisation.

        With kindest regards to your family and yourself,

Letter from Stanley Sedgwick to Tony Stappaerts President of the Antwerp Motor Union.

19

Harvey Hine describes the Antwerp Motor Union as: "the most extraordinary hospitable Society, they had their own club in the middle of town and we were all staying at this hotel by the docks and we had been invited to numerous parties and having prepared our cars and taken the lights, mudguards and wings off, we were then escorted with police escorts to various parties around Antwerp. We went belting down these cobbled streets".

Later, in Ghent, mention must be made of Monsieur Mahy who put a cordoned off section of the Fiat Garage he owned at the disposal of the Bentleys for several years. This garage had previously been a circus and the Bentleys ranged around the ring must have presented quite a sight.

Dick Moss describes it: "That was the garage where they did all the work on the cars and they had a vintage aeroplane hanging down on a big chain and all of the lights were strapped to the wings".

The hospitality received by the Bentley members throughout their time in Belgium, both at Antwerp and later at Ghent, ranging from receptions, cocktail parties to dinners was stupendous – from a cocktail party in 1959 given by a Monsieur Lambrecht, President of "Ecurie Brabo" an Antwerp Motor Club, to, in 1962, another cocktail party arranged this time by a Madame Delcourt, where a participant recalls "a large table was heavily laden with a host of different varieties of food, and every imaginable type of drink was yours for the asking" – Madame was obviously an excellent hostess as well as being an enthusiastic member of the AMU. In 1963 the Mayor of Antwerp gave a Reception in his Parlour "where he plied us with champagne" recalls one attendee, after this the party tottered round the corner to the Restaurant La Rade for cocktails and a cold buffet given yet again by the indefatigable Maurice Rosen, President of the AMU.

In 1964, on the Sunday prior to the Trials, the Bentley party engaged in a tour de force, a different type of trial! It seems firstly a morning cocktail party was given by BP Belgium, this was followed by an afternoon drinks party hosted by the Ford Motor Company of Belgium, to go straight onto the premises of Gaston Stappaerts of the AMU for a superb champagne buffet supper. It was no doubt hoped drivers' livers would stand up to these trials as well as their motors would cope on the morrow!

Edward Barraclough also remembers: "Coming home after these restaurants or night clubs or wherever we had been when we had been out in the cars, no wings, no lights, no nothing and in Antwerp the boulevard was about 4 lanes one way, 4 lanes the other, then a row of trees, and another dual carriageway up the side. Scott Noble took the 8 litre as Frank (Sowden) my father in law always used to go to bed early. Peter (Morley) had his 8 litre and we were coming up to traffic lights. There were about four cars on that lane there and over the other side of the tress on the boulevard there were another two cars. When the lights changed it was a charge of two or three hundred yards to the next set of lights."

Mention must be made of Monsieur and Madame Hettelynk of Ghent who, for the years 1971 to 1974, valiantly gave parties for the Bentley group. Champagne flowed and it is recorded that in 1971 they had invited the group to their little home just for a simple "cocktail and snack". This turned out to be something rather more elaborate. The Review of that year relates "we went into a most beautiful house and onto lawns leading down to a canal where canapés and cocktails were handed out ad lib. Madame H had cleared her lounge and had laid places for 58 people to dine and we all sat down to a first class meal." The Review describes the hospitality as overwhelming as well it might have been with the Bentley group expecting just a single drink and a few nibbles! No wonder the Hettelynk's parties proved so popular in the next few years.

Entertainment was also provided by the Bentley participants themselves. Harvey Hine relates: "Another thing about Ghent and Belgium was Peter Corney's stories, his jokes. Peter Corney had the most incredible repertoire of stories and jokes and his wife Gwenda was even worse. But Peter was very clever because he used to keep a little notebook of all the stories and who he

The President and the Committee of the
Royal Automobile Club of Flanders
The President and the Sport's Committee of the
Royal Automobile Club of Flanders

request the honour of the company of

Mr. Martin Trentham

at the Dinner organised on Friday 21st. May 1976 at the
International Club of Flanders - Gent.
on the occasion of the 10th Flying Kilometer of Gent.
Sint Pieters-Plein - Gent.

8 p.m.
Personal invitation to be
shown at the Entrance.

R.s.v.p. before 15th May 1976
to the Secretary of R.A.C.Fl.
Koopvaardijlaan 49
B-9000 Gent

Evidence of the magnificent hospitality enjoyed by the Bentley participants in Belgium.

had told which story to. So he didn't keep boring you by telling you the same story again. It was absolutely amazing."

David Llewellyn recalls in Antwerp: "The time that Peter Corney and Fred Hoffman went to the nightclub and enjoyed themselves and hadn't got enough money to pay the bill so they decided to keep Peter Corney as a hostage and sent Fred back to the hotel to get some money. In the meantime Peter wanted to "reprocess" some of this expensive booze and they wouldn't let him into the loo on his own, they sent a minder in with him to make sure he did not escape through the window."

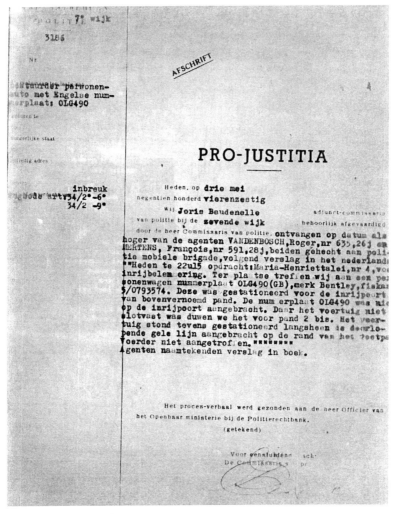

Summons for Club President.

8, Balfour Place,

Park Lane, London, W.1.   3rd June, 1964

Mr. A. Stappaerts,
Antwerp Motor Union,
Lode Ontropstraat 3,
Antwerp,
Belgium.

Dear Tony,

    What have I done? I enclose a document which looks like a
Summons which I have received from the Antwerp police.   I
understand, from a rough translation, that I parked my car in the
wrong place during the prize-giving.   What should I do about this
now?   Have I been fined; should I write to somebody and apologise;
will you deal with it on my behalf, or do I ignore it?

    If I go to Antwerp again, perhaps the police will escort me
for a different purpose!!

                    Kindest regards,

*Letter from Stanley Sedgwick to Tony Stappaerts confessing to Parking misdemeanours
over in Antwerp.*

23

Final Preparations for the Track

So we turn from the partying and jollifications to the serous business of getting ready for the Trials themselves. In 1959 warm up runs were permissible and undertaken as Peter Corney describes "I was then invited to join Stan in a trial run with the Speed Six. Needless to say, I accepted, and before I knew what had hit me, we were blinding along a clear straight road at 125 mph. To one whose previous experience had been limited to a mere 80 mph (downhill in my 3 litre, but only once) 125 mph is, to say the least of it, a totally different kettle of fish. There isn't time to think where you are going because you have already gone past it. On the following day I joined Harold Pounds in a similar run at about 118 mph but this time sans aero screen, sans goggles, sans titfer, and damn near sans coat, pants, tie and passport! Under these conditions I defy anyone to look like anything other than the wrath of God at the end of the run."

Harvey Hine explains the reasoning behind preparing the cars: "On the runs themselves the great thing was to try and keep resistance down, because unlike Brooklands, doing a run in Belgium you had just a flat road and there was always a wind there of one way or another, so trying to achieve speeds against the wind was actually quite difficult. What I had to try and do was to get wind resistance down and the rolling resistance down to the absolute minimum so I fitted a 3/5 axle and then had 525 x 21 tyres pumped up to 65 pounds pressure and took absolutely every ounce of weight off the car that I possibly could."

As part of final fettling for the track, time was spent each year removing wings, lamps, screens, spare wheels and so on in readiness. This was not only a safety precaution but also would make quite an appreciable difference to maximum speed. Jack Bailey reported on the 1963 racing trims in the paddock as follows:-

Rose:	front wings off, rear wings on	(4½ S)
Weston:	all wings on	(4½ S)
Brogden:	sporting replica Le Mans blade type wings (very chic)	(3)
Morley:	no wings	(8)
Burton:	ditto	(8)
Batten:	ditto	(8)
Sowden:	ditto	(8)
Russ Turner:	built on wings	(Mk VI 4½)
Sedgwick:	ordinary road trim	(R. Continental 4.9)

One of the pre runs rituals each year included an official escort through Antwerp to and from various receptions and to the track. Peter Morley relates "we took the Napier out there and at 8 o'clock in the morning they had closed the town of Ghent and with police escort I went through on my own which was rather privileged". "That was the time when they closed the whole town of Ghent and with four outriders and they said to me "would you be able to keep up". "Yes" I said "that will not be a problem". So when we got going on the cobbles they told me to keep up we were doing well over 2000 revs then so I could not resist just touching the throttle and just leaving these coppers. They were all standing on these junctions with guns, you know how they are, whistles blowing and guns waving. You wouldn't see anywhere like that today – the whole town of Ghent closed." Geoffrey Sandwith described what took place in 1965: "Promptly at half past seven that evening our Police Motor Cycle Escort arrived and the cars were lined up to travel two abreast through the streets of Antwerp, no notice was taken of speed limits or of red traffic lights; cross traffic was held up for our passing by one of our escorts. It is doubtful if Royalty in England have ever experienced a drive quite like a Bentley procession at speed through the busy streets of this big city which has a population of nearly two million."

Police escort in Antwerp 1964

Edward Barraclough remembers "these parties and police escorts everywhere in Antwerp – unbelievable – we went underneath a tunnel, under a railway or something and of course everyone was totally uninhibited and played like boy racers, blipped our throttles, that sort of thing". It is good the record shows that after the 1965 event the policeman who had been in charge of Bentley escorts since they first went to Antwerp was presented with an ashtray bearing a model of Harry Rose's Blower Bentley.

Harvey Hine remembers: "Harry Rose was very good to all of us and he used to nanny Rusty Russ Turner; he used to keep him on the straight and narrow. Harry used to go around saying "Got to make sure your car is properly warmed up before you go out on the run. What you have to do is to run it up to get the oil hot so you can hardly put your hand on the engine bearer." He used to go around testing everybody's cars to see if the oil was hot enough before they went out. He was particularly concerned about Rusty "If you don't do that you will break your block". So we all had to make sure our cars were properly warmed up to pass Harry Rose's inspection before we were allowed to go out. He was very good like that." Edward Barraclough tells "I always remember Harry Rose, he wanted things done correctly and properly and he didn't like it if you did not prepare your car properly."

Before the timed speed trials themselves commenced it was of course necessary to fully warm up the Bentleys, which had often been standing idle following their arrival at the track for several hours due to the event running late. Harry Rose, in 1962, enquired about the possibility of obtaining permission to leave the trackside for a short run to warm up his engine, gearbox, transmission and back axle. This presented something of a problem as the regulations did not permit competitors' cars to be driven from the course during the meeting. However the organisers, the ever helpful Antwerp Motor Union, arranged for an official car to be placed at the head and tail of the convoy of Bentleys waiting to compete and warming up duly took place.

So now after a final check on plugs and tyres we are ready for the actual Speed Runs themselves.

Refuelling en route to track at Antwerp in 1962

En route to the track Antwerp 1962

27

The track at Antwerp 1962 – Note lack of Armco!

Saloons lining up to compete at Antwerp 1962.

John Brogden on Start Line at Antwerp in 1962 in JB 833 his 3/4½.

Another shot of the start at Antwerp, this time No. 83 in 1964, Fred Morley in his 4½ Litre.

29

Competing in the wet at Antwerp in 1962.

Racing on the track at Antwerp in 1962. Note the traffic coming in the opposite direction.

Gendarmeries making sure no-one nicks the spare tyres – Antwerp 1962.

Frank Sowden 8 Litre. Fastest Bentley in 1965 at 123.9 m.p.h.

Geoffrey Sandwith's 6½ on the start line at Ghent in 1968.

Paddock scene Ghent 1968. Russ-Turner's ex Birkin Blower in foreground. Note two seater body then fitted.

Trackside at The Trials

"The rules governing record breaking are not generally well known" wrote Stanley Sedgwick in 1965. "The measured distance must be straight and the gradient of the measured section of the road and for one kilometre at each end must not exceed one per cent i.e. 1 in 100. Another rule in the establishment and breaking of records, and this **is** remember the Day of Belgian Records, is that both runs in opposite directions must be completed within 60 minutes."

The organisation and timing of these trials is well described in the BDC Review of July 1962. "Cars were divided into groups of approximately six in number. Each was dispatched from the start at a given signal and on reaching the far end they then made their return run ending up back in the paddock. The second group was then released and returned and so on until all competing cars had completed a run in both directions. The official timing over the measured kilometre was carried out by the RAC of Belgium but a comprehensive signalling system was also in operation handled by an Army Signals Unit. There was a control point for each kilometre of the run – seven kilometres long – and each was in touch with the main control point situated in the paddock. The position of each car as it passed a control point was telephoned back to the main control and plotted on a chart. By this system it was possible to have three cars in action at once with a clear section ahead of each and a considerable saving of time in consequence." Sounds fool proof doesn't it? But Stanley Sedgwick reported in 1965 "During the runs a local motorist determined to exercise what he believed to be his rights as a taxpayer forced his car past marshals guarding the entrance to the course from a side road and proceeded to drive his fully laden vehicle down the length of the whole course. The Clerk of the Course's car left the starting area in hot pursuit loaded with gendarmerie, but I never did hear if they caught the offender!"

Martin Trentham describes his experiences at the Trials: "Having got to Ghent on Saturday morning we drove out to where they were assembled and I still had only about 400 miles on the clock and I was a bit worried about that so I thought I should go and do a few more miles. I set off in the wrong direction as it were on this dual carriageway to do a few more miles and a gendarme popped out of a little box and asked me for my passport, which I thought was a little odd, but I realized afterwards I had actually driven into Holland. So I did a little tour of Holland to get a few more miles on the clock and then back. But because the car had not done anything like 500 miles I didn't feel that I could put my foot flat down. The gearing with the wheels that I had on would have given me 140, but I think my average was 114 or something like that because I didn't want to bust it. It was then back home again the next day, so it was all a bit of a quick trip as far as I was concerned. I don't remember much of the social side of it except there was a sort of a presentation party afterwards. I was looking forward to competing the following year which was 1977 but it was cancelled and that was it, that was the end of the whole thing so I did not have a chance to go flat out."

Peter Morley comments: "Something which comes to my mind when I took the Sunbeam Napier over there with Gordon Russell, with a very high ratio step up gear on it, overdrive, going down the straight just entering the Flying Kilometre and put into top gear at well over 100 mph, all the diff pulled out and it spun round several times, nothing was insured and I noticed that there was traffic on the other side of the road and I thought, well if I was to hit those chaps I would still be doing time! – Only one side of the divided highway of the Autoroute was shut for the Speed Trials, while public continued to use the other side – somewhat unnerving at such close proximity."

Edward Barraclough relates: "I remember standing around on these wind swept long straights, we just enjoyed ourselves standing out in the middle of nowhere. I remember there was a character who came with Jumbo Goddard from Australia. He and Fred Hoffman could smell out a pub, and they said "there's a pub in that wood across about two fields". So at lunchtime when we were not supposed to leave (Stanley would not let us go anywhere at lunch, we had to stand and wait to do our runs) but he went off and did find this pub."

Edward continues: "I didn't do too well on my first trip there because I had one of those old Leston helmets with a visor, with the leather visor sort of thing, like Mike Hawthorn used to race in, and going down the straight it blew off."

Edward has further recollections: "When you are competing, doing the flying mile or something like that, you don't see anything. You just stood with the car parked up and I remember when Harry (Rose) was doing his runs in the blown Team Car; Frank (Sowden) and I had done our runs and we walked across the fields for a mile then crouched down in a ditch near the end of the flying mile. I shall always remember the blower coming down doing about 128 miles per hour. You could see it coming and hear the blower screaming, coming straight towards you and then past, an absolutely fabulous sound – you don't see that anywhere these days – you can't."

There was a major problem with the organisation in 1965 concerning the timing apparatus. There had been serious delays the year before when Stanley Sedgwick was obliged to make a strong complaint. It should be mentioned that the problems were outside the control of the hosts, the Antwerp Motor Union, who had been obliged to leave timing arrangements in the hands of the appropriate Belgian Authority. In the afternoon of the 1965 Trial cars were running three hours late, and there were delays of nearly one and a half hours between being called to the ready and the actual start of the first run. Sedgwick was sufficiently incensed to call "the behaviour of the timekeeping apparatus a disgrace" and he protested in no uncertain terms to the President of the Competition Committee of the Royal Automobile Club of Belgium. The fault lay with the manufacturer of the equipment itself as the letter of 14th December from C V Missotten of the Antwerp Motor Union, reproduced on the following pages makes clear.

One of the major problems of the track itself in 1965 at Antwerp was the insufficient acceleration distance for Bentleys especially. Comparisons of speeds attained in 1965 with those of 6 years earlier at Herentals in 1959 would bear this out. (See Appendix 1 page 57) Sedgwick had written early in 1965 to Tony Stappaerts of the Antwerp Motor Union "I do hope you will do everything possible to extend the acceleration distance at each end of the measured kilometre". Obviously times were affected also a year earlier by this factor. Perhaps it came as a blessing in disguise when Missotten's letter of December 1965 to Stanley Sedgwick reproduced on the following pages goes on to state "the event will not be held this year" that is in 1966 at Antwerp.

So we come to 1967 and a change of venue – to Ghent, Gent, or Gand dependent on whether you are an English or Flemish speaker or a Francophone! The letter produced on page 39 dated 22nd February 1967 from J Lahaye, BP's Racing Services Manager in Belgium, explains the background to the move to Ghent. Rusty Russ Turner, who had by now taken over the helm, was delighted to follow up immediately and contacted the Royal Automobile Club des Flandres. So the whole venture subsequently took place at Ghent for a further ten years.

Ghent had a peculiarity in the arrangements as Dick Moss relates: "When I went in 1968 to Ghent – the toilets were in Holland but the main race meeting was in Belgium, so you had to go through customs every time you wanted to spend a penny!"

Before we move there ourselves it is worth recalling the highlights of the years of racing in Antwerp. In Appendix 1 you will find lists of the results each year, showing the drivers, the Bentleys driven, times and speeds achieved and below each table are footnotes of noteworthy incidents, together with comments by participants. However it was that first year of 1959 at Antwerp when something really special occurred as the next chapter of this work demonstrates.

ANTWERP MOTOR UNION

Antwerpen, 14 th. December, 1965.

Onze ref. :

v.z.w.d.

ALG. SECRETARIAAT
Lode Ontropstraat 3
ANTWERPEN - Tel. (03)38.51.62

Monsieur Stanley Sedgwick.
President of the Bentley Drivers Club.
8, Balfour Place.
Park Lane.
London. W.1.

Dear Mr. Sedgwick,

        Tony is running along like a lion in his cage the last few weeks since he got himself involved in too many automotive organisations. So he allowed me to lay my hand on your last letter and answer it.

        de Harlez's letter leads you , and incidentally us, noway of course.

        As a member of the 'Commission Sportive Nationale' I was involved in a debate where Monsieur Dassy tried desperately to prove that his services were all right and that only Mother Nature had to bear the reponsability of all our misfortunes. Needless to say that it was only too easy for Tony and myself to point out that :

a) the Antwerp Port Authorities acknowledged a wind velocity of Beaufort force 5 which by all means has nothing to do with a Hurricane;

b) too bad if Monsieur Dassy was held at another meeting : is he the only one in this country to be able to make adequate time measurements ?

c) an Antwerp firm, Bell Telephone MfG. C°, member of the I.T.T., with which we entertain the best relation is actually involved in speed measurments of all types of missiles - wind or no wind, sun or no sun - and that their people would be willing to help us in this matter.

        But we felt very soon that it was no use to hurry up matters and therefore we decided to wait

CLUB-HOUSE A.M.U.
Frankrijklei 133
ANTWERPEN - Tel. (03) 31.26.33
Iedere vrijdag 21 uur.

FINANCIELE DIENST
Sterrenlaan 16
WILRIJK - Tel. (03) 49.53.81
P.C.R. 1759.48

Letter from CV Missotten to Stanley Sedgwick acknowledging problems with timing apparatus and difficulty of finding suitable length of road for the Speed Trials.

a little until we find the right opportunity to come back to the matter with success.

Another hitch is the road. We cannot dispose of a proper road for the time being. We need at least a 2.5 kilometer running-in stretch which means a 6 kilometer straight road. As rare as a goddess on earth.

Third and not least, we believe that in severing from the Flying Kilometer for one year, we might awaken a certain intrest not only among our automobile authorities, but also with foreign and belgian competitors which certainly have not shown the same keen intrest as your people always did.

As a conclusion, I may tell you that :

a) the event will not be held this year;

b) we firmly intend to start anew with it as soon as possible, but on an entirely safe basis;

c) this means we first have to be sure of a proper road and with this insight, we are prepared to look elsewhere than around Antwerp. The government is engaged in the construction of true and proper 'autobahn' type of roads which would be all right. By the way, could you accept a time shedule as follows : technical controll on Friday or Saturday evening; immediately afterwards leaving the cars under military controll in a closed paddock (military camp - and maybe anEnglish one) and having the event held next morning between dawn (4 a.m. in june) and 7.30 a.m.

d) we are determined to move the R.A.C.B. to let us have our way about the time keeping and we assure you that we will never dare to invite you again unless we have the irrefutable prove that this matter will be flawless;

e) if we succeed in all this, we will try the utmost to have a larger international participation.

Mrs. Stappaerts and Tony send their kindest regards to you and all their friends of the 'Bentley's', so do I.

Yours sincerely,

Antwerp Motor Union.
C.V. Missotten.

As from: 8 Balfour Place,
Park Lane, London, W.1.   17th December, 1965.

Dear Mr. Missotten,

Thank you very much indeed for rescuing my letter
to Tony and for replying so fully.

The decision not to hold your Speed Trials in 1966
will cause wide disappointment, but I am quite sure that you have made
the right decision.

We must hope that a suitable piece of road will be
available in 1967 and I am sure that you and your colleagues will
spare no efforts to reinstate the event.

You are quite right in thinking that the Flying Kilometer
is the thing to aim for. As far as I know there is no where else in the
world that this is available, whereas there are several opportunities
of doing a Standing Kilometer.

I am quite sure that our members would be prepared
to have their cars scrutineered on Friday or Saturday evening
(preferably Saturday) and to leave them in a closed paddock over night.
They might grumble at having to get up at 3 a.m., but I am quite sure
they would sooner do this than miss the event!

Kindest regards to you, the Stappaerts and all our
friends in the Antwerp Motor Union.

Yours sincerely,

Mr. C.V. Missotten,
Antwerp Motor Union,
Lode Ontropstraat 3,
ANTWERP.

Stanley Sedgwick's reply to Missotten of the AMU.

38

B.M.Russ-Turner
1 North Street,   22nd. Feb.1967
Leatherhead,

Dear Mr. Russ-Turner

 I thank you for your letter of the 14th. Feb,
which had all my attention. The Antwerp Motor Union
is still going strong and this has been proved by
their excellent organisation of the Eurally on
February 18 & 19th.

 Unluckily, they will not be able to organise a
"Day of Records" in 1967; the only and obvious
reason for cancelling the "Flying Kilometer" is that
they were unable to secure a suitable road.
Nevertheless I know they are still looking further
and they have not lost the hope they could arrange
some thing for 1968.

 On the other hand, we just heard that another
Club (Royal Automobile Club des Flandres, 6
Recollettenlei, Gent, Belgium - phone 09 - 256146)
intends to organise the "Kilometre Lance de Gand"
on May 6th. 1967. This will happen on a new road
near Ghent. I have asked the organisers to contact
you directly, and to send you information,
regulations and entry forms.

 Their event will be a national one but open to
all foreign participation. From some information
I received, our national Automobile Club has not
yet given his approval on the state of the road, but
a final decision will be taken this week, so that we
will know definitely if this "Kilometre Lance" goes
on.

     .....over

-2-

 I hope this above mentioned information will
prove useful but do not hesitate to call me if I can
give you more details, about all this.

    Kindest regards,
     Yours sincerely,

      J.Lahaye

     Racing Manager.

*Letter from J. Lehaye, Racing Manager of BP Belgium advising
ending of Speed Trials at Antwerp and commencing new venue at
Ghent.*

As from: 8 Balfour Place,
Park Lane,   28th February, 1967.
London, W.1.

Monsieur J. Lahaye,
International Racing Service
BP Belgium,
162 Jan Van Rijswijcklaan,
ANTWERP -

Dear Mr. Lahaye,

       I was very pleased to hear from Mr. Russ-Turner that the Antwerp Motor Union have not given up their efforts to resume their "Day of Records".

       It is also very interesting to learn that there may be a "Flying Kilometer" near Ghent on the 6th May this year.   Quite by chance I shall be in Ghent this week-end visiting Mr. Mahy's collection of cars.   I shall be staying at the Cour St. Georges Hotel and I hope that it may be possible for me to meet the organising Club and see the proposed road either on Saturday morning or Sunday afternoon.

       I enclose a copy of the letter I am writing to the Royal Automobile Club des Flandres.

       Kindest regards to you and your wife.

       Yours sincerely,

Enc:

Stanley Sedgwick's reply to J Lehaye expressing interest in the new venue at Ghent.

40

Caption: *The Class of 1964 at Antwerp as recorded by John Nutter. Standing L to R: Rusty Russ-Turner, Guy Shoosmith, Harvey Hine, Harold Pounds, Tom Rose, Rupert Glydon, Gary Woodhead, George Burton, Bob Gooda, Frank Sowden, Peter Morley, Fred Morley.*
Sitting L to R: Ann Rose, Edward Barraclough, John Brogden, Clive Russell-Vick, Stanley Sedgwick, Gerry Crozier.

Bentley Boys at Ghent 1967.

41

VLIEGENDE KILOMETER EN KILOMETER STILSTAAND VERTREK
KILOMETRE LANCE ET KILOMETRE DEPART ARRETE DE GAND

Gent - 22 mei 1976

n° Liste des engagés   Lijst der ingeschreven

n°			
11	DECOUTER René	Morris Minni	Duind
12	GEERST Carolus	Simca R II	Duind
14	"JIBY" BAELE Julien	Datsun PE 10	Zimmer
15	"JIBY" BAELE Julien	Datsun 180 Bsss	Zimmer
16	JACKSON Oswald	Peugeot 504 TI	Ros.Bei
17	VAN CAMP Paul	Fiat Lombardi	Excels
18	HOLZ Maurice	Renault R 1173	Scud.To
19	CAUDRON Jean	B M W 2002 T II	E3 Aalst
21	MOERMANS Jean Pierre	V.W. V	Duind
22	VERSCHOORE Philippe	Citroën GSX2	Duind
23	LEBACQ Daniel	Lola 190	Duind
24	LEBACQ Daniel	Toralba	Duind
25	VAN HUFFEL Norbert	Porsche Turbo 930	Duind
26	"JOHN J. CALY" DE BRUYCKER	Unil Sport	Duind
27	DE BRAUWER Jo	MANTA 1,9 L	Duind
28	"RIALTO" LAUTE Dirk	V.W. Golf	Duind
29	MARLIER R.	Porsche Carrera	Duind
31	VAN HUFFEL Alain	Alfa Roméo Sud TI	Duind
32	VAN HUFFEL Jean	Iso Rivolta	Duind
33	EMBO Marc		Duins
34	"MICHOU" Vandermispel	V.W. Polo	Duind
35	HAERENS Jozef	Peugeot 404	Ros.Be
36	SOUSSI	Alpine 1600	Duind
37	CALLEWAERT Gaby	Opel Manta	Groeni
38	CLAES Freddy	Simca R II	Ros.Be
39	DERIDDER Ludo	Datsun PE 10	Zimmer
42	DEDAPPER Armand	Simca R II	Draak
43	CRUYT Christian	Toyota Carina	Duind
44	PRILS Marc "SPILLE"	Honda S800	Gh.Rac
45	TOORRE Walter	Datsun 120 Asss	Gh.Rac
46	WINSEL Patrick	Lotus Europa	British
47	BELL Derek	.Ferrari 512M	Gh.Rac
48	VAN DEN BROECK Erwin	B.M.W. 1600	Duind
49	"JOHN J. CALY" DE BRUYCKER	Alfa Roméo 1300	Duind
51	FRANCHOO Stephan	Simca R II	Duind
52	MAERTENS Léon	Alfa Roméo 1300	Duind
53	DEPONDT Joost	Audi 100	Duind
54	VAN HAECKE Freddy	Alfa Roméo Sud	Duind
55	RULENS. Pierre	de Tomaso Panth.	Tois Or
41	BARLOW David	Ferrari 246	British
56	PARAGE Yves	Autobianchi Abarth	Gaume
57	MOROBE Christian	Austin Cooper	Duind
58	VERNAEVE Julien	Triuph Dolom.	
4	BAETENS Patrick	Ducati - Moto	M.C.G.
3	DE CLERCQ	Suzuki - Moto	M.C.G.
2	STEFENS Peter	Kawasaki - Moto	M.C.G.
1	VERSPEELT	Norton - Moto	M.C.G.

Official List of some of the entrants of the Speed Trials at Ghent in 1976 which shows many marques other than Bentley participated in these events.

42

ROYAL AUTOMOBILE CLUB DES FLANDRES

10° KILOMETRE LANCE DE GAND - 22 Mai 1976

86	"JUMBO"	BENTLEY 1928		16"54	217.654	135·3
69	"RUSTY"		1929	17"69	203.504	126·5
76	WILCOCK F.M.		1930	18"47	194.910	
77	GAUNTLETT Vicotor		1974	19"13	188.186	
73	GAUNTLETT Jean		1939	19"14	188.087	
79	TRENTHAM Martin		1948	19"66	183.112	113·8
71	GAUNTLETT Victor		1929	21"90	164.383	
75	SHOOSMITH Ann		1928	22"52	159.857	
85	GUPPY John		1975	22"65	158.940	
82	PARKINSON Barry		1928	23"61	152.477	
83	TEAL Charles		1952	24"71	145.690	90·5
84	"BOB"		1	29"96	120.160	
81	"DON"		1924	31"61	113.888	

10° KILOMETRE ARRETE de GAND

86	"JUMBO"	Bentley 1928		26"82	134.228	83·4
85	GUPPY John		1975	29"57	121.745	
76	WILCOCK F.Michael		1930	30"07	119720	
79	TRENTHAM Martin		1948	30"84	116.731	72·5
69	"RUSTY"		1929	31"24	115.236	
73	GAUNTLETT Jean		1939	31"26	115.163	
77	GAUNTLETT Victor		1939	31"26	115.163	
71	GAUNTLETT Victor		1929	34"43	104.559	
83	TEALL Charles		1952	34"82	103.388	
75	SHOOSMITH Ann		1928	35"41	101.666	
82	PARKINSON B.H.		1928	38"03	94.662	
84	"BOB"		1	39"62	90.863	
81	"DON		1924	46"	78.260	

Official Results for Bentleys at Ghent in 1976 issued by Royal Automobile Club des Flandres.

Forrest Lycett and 1959

It has been described earlier how, in 1959, Stanley Sedgwick approached Forrest to compete at Ghent in his 8 litre "to improve upon your 1950 times at Jabbeke". But Forrest was not all that keen initially. When Stanley made a further attempt to persuade him, Forrest was ready for him with a cunning ploy. "I've come to regard the Jabbeke project as quite a good thing but unfortunately my tyres are old and consequently unsafe for high speed: furthermore, being of obsolete dimensions, it is not possible to procure suitable replacements" and "that's the last I'll hear of that" Forrest chuckled to himself until a month later Stanley resumed the assault to persuade him to join the venture. "Since last speaking to you I've been in touch with Dunlops. They promise to make, specially for you, tyres to your requirements and what's more guarantee them safe up to 150 mph". Forrest realised he'd been cornered and must get on with the job. He contacted Don Mackenzie, son of the late L Mackenzie ("Mac") to collect his 8 litre asking him to go through the car end to end with the aim of making it faster than it had ever been. Forrest's only constraint was that the engine must come within the official B class (under 8000 cc). Forrest knew "that would entail its first rebore and linering back to 110 mm bore as the 8 litre engine starts life so near to 8000 cc there remains little margin for subsequent cylinder wear". So Forrest joined the first venture to Ghent in 1959 and, as the Summary of Speeds and Times in the appendix shows, the 8 litre breathed on by Don Mackenzie with Forrest at the wheel achieved the following splendid results:-

141.121 mph and 140.515 mph, a mean of 140.845 mph for the two flying mile runs, and
141.667 mph and 140.510 mph, a mean of 141.131 mph for the two flying kilometre runs.

This was perhaps marred somewhat as Forrest himself related "succumbing to the temptation to have just one more 'go', in the course of it I ran out of petrol, the resultant weakened mixture burning a hole in a piston crown". In spite of this the car returned to London on five cylinders. This mishap caused by lack of fuel was to an extent the result of Forrest earlier driving a 15 mile warm up and the fact that Don Mackenzie had spent the morning driving up and down the road parallel to the track with a supply of fuel only to be passed by the 8 litre going flat out the other way, or arriving at the turning point just after Forrest took off in the other direction! In spite of this Forrest gained the Belgian National Class B Record and beat the Facel Vega's previous record when driven by Maurice Trintignant.

By 1959 Forrest had been a Bentley owner for over 35 years – devoting much thought, time and finance to experimental work to improve the performance of his Bentleys. At the time of his record breaking at Antwerp in 1959 he was suffering from serious physical discomfort caused by his arthritis in his hands. It says much of his courage and character that he said nothing of the pain he suffered whilst driving. As Stanley Sedgwick wrote "Forrest Lycett's performance in his 8 litre would have called for the highest praise if he had been young and in robust health; as it was it was magnificent. There is not a member of the Bentley Drivers Club who would not count himself fortunate indeed to be able to drive nearly as well at an age many years his junior. Outside immediate Club circles the fact that an elderly gentleman could drive an elderly car at such a speed is considered little short of miraculous and evokes the highest admiration. Forrest Lycett not only owned the fastest vintage Bentley in the world (in 1959) but could justly have claimed to be the only septuagenarian in the world to have been timed at over 140 mph." A fitting tribute to a gallant gentleman and his superb 8 litre Bentley, whose performance deserves to be singled out especially.

Forrest Lycett's 8 Litre built by Don Mackenzie in its final form in 1957/8 with black body & wheels and maroon mudguards.

45

'WO' presenting Forrest Lycett with an award at Dorchester Hotel, London in the 1950's.

Forrest at the wheel of his fabulous 8 Litre probably at BDC Silverstone in the 1950's.

Forrest at speed.

'Jumbo' Jet in 1972

John Goddard had been coming to Ghent since 1968 but each year had suffered problems with his 3/8 litre Bentley. In 1968, on arrival at the paddock, the petrol tank was found to be leaking badly. "The tank was emptied completely and a repair was effected with a glass fibre provided by Harry Rose and applied by glass fibre exponent John Brogden", the BDC Review of that year reports: "The repair was left to harden before refilling the tank in the hope the seam would not open up on pressurising the tank. This means of raising petrol to the carburettors was used extensively for racing in the vintage years and those who have studied Bentley team cars will have

'Jumbo' Goddard

observed the hand pump on the dashboard." John had waited five years for this day, the last time he drove the car in Belgium being prior to supercharging modifications. He was to be disappointed; on his first run, before he was out of sight, misfiring could be heard – "alas the application of a mere 2 lb/sq in air pressure produced a petrol leak and the pressure on the gauge falling to zero at 3000 rpm in top gear, indicating fuel starvation of the biggest possible manner". So frustratingly ended the 3/8 litre's participation in the 1968 event.

In 1969 John was again disappointed in spite of achieving an average of 120.85 mph on the two runs – he broke a piston on the return run and merely coasted over the finish line on his second run.

His Bentley and name do not feature in the 1970 Ghent Speed Trials but he was back there the following year of 1971 achieving a mean average speed of 126 mph for his two runs – the fastest of all the Bentleys present, but yet again beset by problems of clutch slip and burning a hole in No.5 piston described by the Review writer that year as "this to John is a mere fleabite"; but how frustrating that he had yet again been unable to demonstrate the Bentley's true potential.

So we come to the 1972 Trials and the BDC Review of that June sums up John 'Jumbo' Goddard's achieving the results he had been aiming for so doggedly over the past years. "On Saturday 6th May on the Kennedy Iaan Highway near Ghent, in windswept and generally adverse conditions, 65 years old John with his turbo-charged 3/8 Bentley succeeded in creating a new record for the flying kilometre of a fantastic 158.2 miles per hour, thus beating by a handsome margin the late Forrest Lycett's record of 141.131 mph in 1959." The disappointing set backs of previous years at Ghent had been overcome by sheer determination and hard work. John modestly referred to his success as "mainly an engineering exercise!". It was in fact back in 1962 when he had achieved 136.4 mph for the flying kilometre that a friend from the Garrett Corporation suggested more speed might result from fitting a pair of Garrett Exhaust Turbo Chargers. John accepted this and put the work in the hands of Don McKenzie and his partner Douglas Guppy, who with the then young John Guppy of Blandford are entitled to share full credit for the results achieved in 1972.

In 1972, on the day, the 8 litre engine was fitted with boost dump valves, to restrict the supercharge to 'safe' limits, and special Firestone 750 x 20 rear racing tyres with sticky compound treads. We are indebted to Bill Cheston, as a witness, for a description of Jumbo's run: "We had assembled at a point 100 metres from the start line of the flying kilo, which was about 3 kilos from the actual standing start – we estimated that at this point the Bentleys would be going at maximum speed. The wind blew force 5 across the track; it was cold and had been raining. It is difficult to judge speed differentials at such close proximity but the next car (the 3/8 litre) certainly made an effect. Green, low, and Oh! so very fast on approach. Even at one kilo distant it was much faster than the others. Then at 500 metres away, across the intersecting road protected by barriers twenty five feet apart and seeming so narrow with people hanging all over them, a moment when at 160 miles per hour in a 45 year old 'new' car, the weak hearted would have lifted off for fear of hitting a spectator ambling about. No lift off for Jumbo though. A never to be forgotten sight, a flash, a millisecond as he passed, frozen images in one's memory, of a profile, a chin jutting out from under a helmet; hands clutching the wheel so hard, and a blue boiler suit that had probably stoked boilers in the China Sea, billowing up with air pressure, the only restraint to his incredible run. Towards the finish his speed was such that 120 yards from the end of the road he was still doing the same in mph. A final snap from the brakes, a whiff of Firestone smoke and the car was back in the paddock with the tach tell-tale showing 4000 rpm." John Proctor recalls Jumbo telling him after it was all over that at over 150 mph the steering became very light and the Bentley was difficult to steer with the front wheels lifting and barely touching the road surface.

Harvey Hine corroborates this: "Jumbo Goddard brought his turbo charged 3/8 and he was absolutely extraordinary as on the return trip there was a slight bend at the end in Ghent and he was going about 170 and he said the car was actually lifting off and when he got to this bend he hadn't got any steering, it was so light the car was taking off! He said he was actually very frightened when he got back. So that was a bit alarming."

Bill Cheston's and John Proctor's descriptions evoke the atmosphere and scene of John Goddard's historic runs – an incredible achievement – the Bentley must have exceeded 160 mph on its return run. What a fitting tribute to one man's dogged persistence, sheer courage and complete trust in those who were responsible for the advanced engineering under the bonnet – resulting in the highest speed of the 1972 Ghent Trials of any entrant, vintage or modern, and the fastest a Bentley of any age had ever travelled before.

So what of this remarkable driver. At a gathering at Dick and Ann Moss' home early in 2010 Bentley drivers at those now far off Trials fondly remembered, in

'Jumbo' and his record breaking machine.

conversation with Alan Bodfish from the W O Bentley Memorial Foundation, the out-of-the-ordinary somewhat larger than life characters Jumbo kept company with.

Edward Barraclough recalls one individual, a Campbell Jacquet, a friend of Jumbo's: "He had a glass eye and would go into a bar and order a couple of drinks and he would take the glass eye out and pop it in the glass." Harvey Hine: "He used to put it on the mantelpiece until his wife came in, and she would say "Put your glass eye back", because it was unpleasant to other people. He would then dip it into his beer and put it back into his eye."

Edward Barraclough: "He was a very dry Australian who had about 40,000 sheep and said "it's an absolute bugger finding names for them all". Harry Rose and Jumbo used to get together, they used to sit together and score points off each other. I'll always remember in the hotel before an evening cocktail party or something Harry would say "Are you going to have a shower or bath?" He said "Why do you think I'm dirty?"

Peter Morley: "Jumbo never sent anything to the laundry; he just put new shirts on or everything in the dustbin and put on a new shirt or pair of socks." Edward Barraclough: "Very rarely did he wear socks". Alan Bodfish: "Didn't he wear the same pair of shoes for years and years?" Harvey Hine: "Yes, he had the same blazer he had when he was 21, it was all ragged but he would not buy a new one and it was double breasted to start with but he had to keep altering the buttons on it. And he only ever had one pair of socks and when they got so smelly he had to send them to the cleaners and then he would walk around with no socks on until he got them back." Dick Moss: "So with the shirt, he would put one on until it was dirty and then throw it in the dustbin". Peter Morley: "He would then get a new one from Marks and Spencers or somewhere like that".

Tom Rose: "He never had a normal car – did he?" Edward Barraclough: "I remember his wife out in Australia who had to go out shopping in some supercharged Mini-Cooper with racing cams and God knows what. She found it very very difficult and said "I don't know why Jumbo can't get a normal car." Tom Rose: "He had a very nice 3 Litre Sunbeam from 1923". Alan Bodfish: "Didn't he have a rather obscure French make called a Cottin-Degoutte?" Harvey Hine: "He used to park that in my garage at Silverstone, he used to leave it there when he was in England doing something. I always had to have a bottle of Rum in the house when Jumbo called. He only ever drank neat Rum with a chunk of lemon in it – that was it Navy Rum."

Conclusions

The high spots of the Speed Trials in Belgium between 1959 and 1976 were, to my mind, undoubtedly those at Antwerp in the first year 1959 with Forrest Lycett's record breaking runs in his 8 litre, and 1972 at Ghent with that record superseded by Jumbo Goddard in his 3/8 achieving timed runs approaching 160 mph. I make no apology for describing these in greater detail in the previous two chapters. For other years it is necessary to turn to Appendix 1 & 2 which list by year all the participants, their Bentleys, the timings and speeds achieved together with 'snippets' worthy of note, reported comments by those involved and details of ailments occurring to entrants' Bentleys.

We have explained why the Trials at Antwerp were obliged to cease in 1965 but why did the Ghent series terminate in 1976? This is not made clear in any Review article of the time that I can find. I believe a number of factors contributed. Accepting that John Goddard's achievements of 1972 were the peak – perhaps years after were something of an anticlimax. In the year following of 1973 Bill Cheston's report in the BDC Review is entitled "The Battle of Crewe" – the action centring around those models with only a sprinkling of vintage Bentleys – one 3 litre, one 4½ and one Speed 6. Four members entered Crewe cars. (In 1972 seven vintage Bentleys participated.) This led Rusty Russ Turner to write in the 1973 Review: "The event really is worthy of better support from Bentley enthusiasts generally. Belgium is the only place in Europe at the moment where heavy motor cars such as ours can wind up safely for a true top speed burst" – he goes on to add "The Bentley Spirit was not bred by static Bentleys in garages and museums, but by Bentleys used on the roads and in competition". Hear, hear - I humbly echo his sentiments. Rusty's words had some effect since in 1974 a total of eight Bentleys took part at Ghent and nine were there in 1975. In the final year the number increased to 14 Bentleys due, I suspect, to it being urged on members to participate it being the 10th Anniversary of the event at Ghent, and indeed the 400th Anniversary of the Independence of Belgium from the Spaniards. It was also billed as being the 40th Anniversary of the inaugural run of the newly formed Bentley Drivers Club to Hurley back in 1936. In spite of the increased attendance, 1976 was the last Speed Trial at Ghent in which it appears Bentleys took part. I suspect, however, factors outside the control of the BDC were also responsible, at least in part; this being the era of devaluation of sterling, the three day week, rubbish uncollected in the streets, corpses remaining unburied due to industrial action and general economic malaise which must have affected BDC members' finances, as was the case with most other citizens of the UK at that time.

Significantly I suspect it was also becoming increasingly difficult for the RAC des Flandres to find a suitable length of track for Bentleys to compete on. In 1972 Jumbo Goddard had barely the distance required to pull up at the end of the measured mile. Finding a sufficient length of road to meet the regulations had earlier been a problem at Antwerp causing the Trials to terminate there in 1965. It also must have become nigh on impossible to close a section of the motorway anywhere in Belgium with the increasing density of traffic everywhere. Perhaps this was the true reason for the end of Bentleys ten year participation at Ghent?

How can this period of the Trials in Belgium be summed up? Back in September 1959, following the first venture at Antwerp, the Bentley Drivers Club President, Stanley Sedgewick, wrote in his musings on the event that year: "I would like to put on record the wonderful spirit of cooperation and sportsmanship that characterised the whole venture. The way in which a number of chaps of widely differing temperaments, ages and means worked together as a team without any ructions is a tribute to the single mindedness imbued in enthusiasts by vintage Bentleys. Knowledge, effort, tools were pooled for the good of all." I believe Rusty Russ Turner could, in 1976, have written in similar vein.

Harvey Hine sums it up well: "There wasn't any competition between ourselves so much on the Flying Kilometre but there was a lot of competition in the wine bar and club." When asked to elaborate Harvey replied:" I don't think it's publishable!"

I like to think such a spirit of generosity and comradeship lies at the centre of the Club and its members worldwide to this very day early in the twenty first century, as I write, a decade short of a century since the sound of the first 3 litre engine was first heard in that mews off Baker Street in 1919.

It is a real credit so many members of the Club took their Bentleys, some year after year, to Belgium to 'have a go' and achieve the results they did.

Tom Rose concludes: "My memory of my trips to both Ghent and Antwerp were of a fabulous, fabulous weekend. It was just bloody good fun, it really was".

W. O. would certainly have approved and been quietly amazed at what his creations of several decades earlier were still capable of in the hands of true devotees of the marque bearing his name.

OLD BENTLEY DRIVER

By RED DANIELLS
(with abject apologies to
Charles Lutwidge Dodgson)

"You're an old Bentley driver," the young man said,
"And minus your spectacles, blind.
Yet you persistently drive at the ton -
You have got to be out of your mind."

"At Brooklands we motored," the old man recalled,

"Over pot-holes for hundreds of miles
With only some small loss of fillings from teeth
And attacks of the Chalfont St. Giles."

"That may be," said the youth, "but you've now reached an age

When most men sit quietly indoors.
Yet through Belgium you blast in excess of the ton
In that rattling old hot-rod of yours."

"A mere stroll," said the sage. "A motor like this

Can be safely relied on to win.
You'd be unwise to try in your modern device Constructed of plastic and tin."

By Red Daniells -from "Bentley Golden Jubilee Book 1986".

Stanley Sedgwick being presented with The Bardahl Cup for the "Most Representative" Club at Antwerp 1962.

"Jaguar Pressé?" – with apologies to Brockbank.
Other cars such as the Le Mans 'D' Type Jaguar of Jacques De Clippel, competed and is shown in front of Johnty Williamson's Bentley at Antwerp 1962.

The following Appendices, One and Two on pages 57 to 73, detail the results of the Speed Trials at Antwerp from 1959 to 1965 and then at Ghent from 1967 to 1976. There was no involvement by Bentleys in Belgium Speed Trials in 1966 as the text has earlier explained. The tables show participants, their Bentleys and speeds achieved each year and these tables are reproduced from the actual records produced after each trial in their original printed format; hence the lack of symmetry in type size, style and layout. I apologise to those readers who wish to study the figures therein in detail if they are obliged as I am to wield a magnifying glass to read the contents more easily.

Appendix One

SPEED RESULTS BY YEAR

SPEED TRIAL RESULTS AT ANTWERP 1959
Summary of Participating Drivers, their Bentleys Speeds and Times.

Vintage Bentleys at Antwerp

May 26, 1959

SUMMARY OF SPEEDS AND TIMES

FLYING				A to H m.p.h.	H to A m.p.h.	Mean m.p.h.
Lycett	....	8 litre	Mile	141.121	140.515	140.845
			Km.	141.667	140.510	141.131
Batten	....	8 litre	Mile	123.626	123.203	123.414
			Km.	124.204	122.975	123.587
Sedgwick	....	6¼ litre	Mile*	128.663	126.984	127.818
			Km.**	128.781	126.954	127.897
Sears	....	4¼ litre(s)	Mile	125.698	124.869	125.304
			Km.	126.380	124.759	125.599
Pounds	....	4¼ litre	Mile	119.244	118.733	119.008
			Km.	119.750	No time	————
Rose	....	4¼ litre	Mile	108.991	109.589	109.289
			Km.	109.065	109.815	109.439
Llewellyn	....	3 litre	Mile	100.027	96.982	98.495
			Km.	99.952	97.131	98.543

* Sedgwick driving.   ** Burton driving.

A to H—Antwerp to Herentals (i.e. West to East)
H to A—Herentals to Antwerp (i.e. East to West)

STANDING				A to H secs.	H to A secs.	Mean secs.
Lycett	....	8 litre	Mile	38.68	37.76	38.22
			Km.	—	27.04	————
Batten	....	8 litre	Mile	41.44	41.68	41.56
			Km.	30.63	29.79	30.21
Sedgwick	....	6¼ litre	Mile	45.78	46.13	45.95
			Km.	32.65	32.49	32.57
Sears	....	4¼ litre(s)	Mile	43.90	44.55	44.22
			Km.	31.52	32.12	31.82
Pounds	....	4¼ litre	Mile	43.47	43.08	43.27
			Km.	30.11	30.60	30.35
Rose	....	4¼ litre	Mile	45.87	46.19	46.03
			Km.	32.83	32.79	32.81
Llewellyn	....	3 litre	Mile	48.79	49.11	48.95
			Km.	—	34.61	————

E

1959 Antwerp 'Snippets'

George Burton suffered a dropped cylinder liner on No 3, which lay in fragments in the sump. He was unable to make even one high speed run.

Forrest Lycett ran short of petrol and the resultant lean mixture burnt out a piston after his earlier record breaking runs.

David Llewellyn achieved over 100 mph in his 3 litre on one way on the Mile Run! But he just missed the 100 mph mean record for both runs. This was with a 3 litre engine built by Don MacKenzie which replaced David's then 3 litre sporting a 4½ bottom end.

David Llewellyn writes himself about his performance at Antwerp 1959: "At that time I still owned 3-litre OL 5099, which I had built from bits of cars which had been broken up. It was probably one of the fastest 3-litres ever. I was asked to take it to Antwerp, and accepted.

Someone then pointed out to Stan Sedgwick that my engine was not exactly "standard". My engine was the same as the Pacey Hassan, pre-war, when in 3-litre form, except that my engine was not blown. It did have a 4½ crankshaft, and pistons that were very tall above the top ring. My pistons were made, by Brooklands Engineering, from the same patterns as the Pacey Hassan, but reduced in height a bit as I was running on petrol not methanol.

Anyway, Stan decided that I ought to have a more standard engine, and Don McKenzie kindly offered to lend me his as it was out of his car at the time. So I duly drove up to Thornton Heath one morning, and we took my engine out and put his in.

My clutch operating arrangements were different from Don's, so we had to fit his brake pedal shaft. So I drove to Thornton Heath with a central throttle pedal, and drove back the same car, the same day, with the throttle on the outside. Quite interesting!

Jack Williamson also lent me a high ratio axle; on the clear understanding that I would use Castrol 'R' as the only lubricant. Castrol 'R' is like a certain beer, and reaches the parts other oils do not reach. I still think it is by far the best lubricant for vintage Bentley axles, except the hypoid axle on the 8-litre.

The car did just over 100 mph in one direction, but just less than 100 mph on the average of two runs. Don's engine was noticeably less powerful than mine, so it would be interesting to know what "OL" would have done with her own engine. Engine and axle were returned to their respective owners with no damage, and much thanks.

W.O. subsequently asked me why they achieved 100 mph in a 3-litre in the twenties, and I did not. I said "too much frontal area". Yes he said you are right. "OL" had a homemade body which was made for comfortable touring rather than top speed.

BENTLEYS AT ANTWERP

Timed Kilometres

	1962		1959	
	Flying M.p.h.	*Standing Secs.*	*Flying M.p.h.*	*Standing Secs.*
Goddard (3/8)				
A — H	137·997	28·00		
H — A	134·269	28·27		
Mean	136·149	28·13		
Batten (8)				
A — H	124.828	32.68	*124·205*	*30·63*
H — A	118·105	30·53	*122·976*	*29·79*
Mean	121·374	31·60	**123·587**	**30·21**
Burton (3/4½)				
A — H	118·670	29·56	*104·529**	
H — A	113·896	30·13		
Mean	116·264	29·84		
Pounds (4½)				
A — H	115·903	30·91	*119·750**	*30·11*
H — A	112·014	30·92		*30·60*
Mean	114·012	30·91		**30·35**
Sedgwick (R-Type Cont.)				
A — H	111·234	34·92		
H — A	108·326	34·93		
Mean	109·760	34·92		
Rose (4½)				
A — H	110·085	33.10	*109·065*	*32·79*
H — A	108·694	32·94	*109·815*	*32·83*
Mean	109·385	33·02	**109·722**	**32·81**
Brogden (3)				
A — H	91·191	34·60		
H — A	87·006	35·25		
Mean	89·049	34·92		
Morten (3/4½)				
A — H	85·837	33·42		
H — A	88·381	38·00		
Mean	87·107	35·71		
Williamson (3)				
A — H	55·881	40·09		
H — A	60·869	42·99		
Mean	58·268	41·54		
Lycett (8)				
A — H			*141·667*	
H — A			*140·511*	*27·04**
Mean			**141·131**	
Sedgwick (6½)				
A — H			*128·781*	*32·65*
H — A			*126·954*	*32·49*
Mean			**127·897**	**32·57**
Sears (4½S)				
A — H			*126·380*	*31·52*
H — A			*124·759*	*32·12*
Mean			**125·599**	**31·82**
Llewellyn (3)				
A — H			*99·952*	
H — A			*97·173*	*34·61**
Mean			**98·543**	

A — H = Antwerp to Herentals
H — A = Herentals to Antwerp
* = Run in one direction only

1962 Antwerp 'Snippets'

'Rusty' Russ Turner threw a No 3 big end during the final kilometre of his run but not before he had covered the measured distance at around 110 mph.

Rusty proceeded in the hotel garage with his mechanic to drop the sump, remove the con rod, lift the head and remove the piston and all other necessary parts to allow his car to proceed on 5 cylinders – some achievement in running repair work during the event!

SPEED TRIAL RESULTS AT ANTWERP 1963

RESULTS (B.D.C. Members)

		Time, seconds		
		Mile	Kilometer	½-Mile
Crozier	Mercedes 300 S.L.	40.70	29.19	18.15
Sedgwick	R Continental 4.9-litre	48.61	34.33	
Gooda	Rolls-Royce Silver Cloud	46.63	32.98	17.92
Brogden	3-litre	56.29	39.35	20.94
Weston	4½-litre	46.85	33.53	17.91
Morten	4½-litre	43.02	30.11	15.54
Rose	4½-litre (S)	45.00	32.00	17.44
Batten	8-litre	44.92	32.33	
Russ-Turner	Mk. VI 4½-litre	47.44	33.61	18.02
Morley (Charles)	8-litre	43.25		
Sowden	8-litre	42.54	30.75	16.71
Burton	8-litre (see report)	56.14		

The above results are the mean of two runs in opposite directions. The time in seconds, rather than the mean speed in miles or kilometres per hour has been given, as being of more significance to readers.

1963 Antwerp 'Snippets'

George Burton's 8 litre suffered on the day before the trial the seizure of a brand new blower, which broke the driving chain. Fred Hoffmann and Donald McKenzie missed all the parties that day to work on the car, assisted by Gerry Crozier and Bob Gregory and it was repaired by the next day for it to run. Alas the blower did it again. However the rotor having stopped in a position where there was a good path for the gases from the carburettors to the ports, George finished both his runs – returning so he thought out of it, with no crash hat and smoking a pipe, but having been timed discovered he'd won a trophy.

Morley had a piston grab in the mile run so didn't compete in the kilometre.

Oliver Batten was forced to withdraw with his clutch refusing to disengage.

				Flying Kilometre			Standing Kilometre		
				M.p.h.	M.p.h.	Mean M.p.h.	Secs.	Secs.	Mean Secs.
BENTLEYS									
Class 14 (4,000 c.c.–5,000 c.c.)									
70	L. Rose	R. Cont.	... ...	97·896	111·179	104·140	—	—	—
71	S. Sedgwick	R. Cont.	... ...	96·419	109·225	102·424	35·38	34·36	34·87
Class 15 (Over 5,000 c.c.)									
73	B. M. Russ-Turner	Mk. VI(S)	... ...	92·472	114·832	104·334	33·01	30·94	31·97
74	A. R. Gooda	S3 Cont.	... ...	108·800	120·200	114·246	32·81	31·43	32·12
Class 7 (2,000 c.c.–3,000 c.c.)									
77*	G. W. Woodhead	3	... ...	71·103	84·032	77·029	41·43	37·78	39·60
79*	H. P. Hine	3	... ...	89·263	92·703	90·969	34·64	34·12	34·38
Class 8 (3,000 c.c.–5,000 c.c.)									
67	Miss W. A. Rose	3½	... ...	84·508	92·206	88·207	37·89	36·20	37·04
80*	R. Glydon	3/4½	... ...	81·610	89·945	85·574	40·92	39·01	39·96
81*	W. F. J. Brogden	3/4½	... ...	92·206	100·221	96·406	34·04	32·27	33·15
83*	F. Morley	4½	... ...	95·188	103·466	99·154	34·69	33·63	34·16
84*	C. C. Russell Vick	4½	... ...	74·390	87·380	80·378	41·67	38·21	39·94
85*	H. S. Pounds	4½	... ...	99·863	117·547	108·012	32·48	30·37	31·42
Class 9 (5,000 c.c.–8,000 c.c.)									
89*	G. H. G. Burton	3/5.6	... ...	103·753	111·235	107·390	29·98	29·42	29·70
90*	H. Rose	4½(S)	... ...	81·759	91·043	86·168	—	—	—
92*	F. P. Morley	8	... ...	94·465	120·071	105·765	30·92	29·57	30·24
93*	G. Shoosmith	6½	... ...	80·263	103·370	90·381	37·53	35·94	36·73
94*	F. A. Sowden	8	... ...	114·479	123·043	118·607	30·40	29·99	30·19
OTHER MAKES									
Class 7 (1,000 c.c.–1,150 c.c.)									
33*	G. M. Crozier	Austin Cooper S	...	91·415	100·131	95·595	34·92	32·30	33·61
Class 7 (2,000 c.c.–3,000 c.c.)									
78*	T. D. L. Rose	Aston Martin DB3S	...	120·394	136·315	127·897	28·51	26·68	27·59
Class 8 (3,000 c.c.–5,000 c.c.)									
82*	J. E. Barraclough	Jaguar XK 120C	...	133·627	107·390	119·112	24·72	23·36	24·04
91	G. H. G. Burton	Type 59 Bugatti(S)	...	128·190	139·373	133·548	—	—	—
95*	W. A. Taylor	Type 59 Bugatti(S)	...	109·332	128·633	118·231	27·98	25·46	26·72

Cars marked * completed their Flying Kilometre runs in pouring rain on a very wet road.
The remaining Flying Kilometre runs and *all* the Standing Kilometre runs were completed in fine weather on a dry road.
A strong cross-wind was blowing throughout *all* Flying and Standing Kilometre runs.

1964 Antwerp 'Snippets'

Harry Rose had two very disappointing runs on his Blower; the car popping and banging during his kilometre run. The centre electrodes of the plugs on number 2 & 3 cylinders were completely burnt out, due it was later discovered to insufficient fuel being delivered by the twin pumps at over 3,500 rpm.

George Burton was plagued with carburation troubles but nevertheless managed a mean average of 107.4 mph – not bad for the first time out for this rebuilt engine.

John Proctor in 2010 wrote: "In the late spring of 1964 Bob Gooda, who was Chairman of our local Motor Club, invited me to attend the Belgium Day of Records at Antwerp in May on that year. I thoroughly enjoyed the event and was amazed at the very generous hospitality of the Antwerp Motor Union and its Chairman Tony Stappaerts". John echoes the comments of others earlier in this work.

RESULTS

		Flying Kilometre			
		Westwards m.p.h.	Eastwards m.p.h.	Average m.p.h.	Remarks
BENTLEYS					
Group III (Grand Touring Cars)—Class 14 (4,000 c.c. to 5,000 c.c.)					
72	J. H. BAILEY ... ... Mk. VI	83·3	90·0	86·5	
	Group IV (Sports Cars)—Class 14 (4,000 c.c. to 5,000 c.c.)				
81	D. G. SILCOCK ... ... R. Cont. (4·6)	—	106·8	—	Westward Run not timed
82	S. SEDGWICK ... ... R. Cont. (4·9)	97·6	106·7	101·9	1964 = 102·4
83	G. R. SANDWITH 4½	75·5	84·8	79·9	
	Group IV (Sports Cars)—Class 15 (5,000 c.c. to 8,000 c.c.)				
85	J. R. NUTTER 6½	89·0	95·9	92·3	
86	A. R. GOODA ... ... S3 Cont.	111·9	116·9	114·4	1964 = 114·2
	Group V (Racing Cars)—Class 7 (2,000 c.c. to 3,000 c.c.)				
89	J. D. SMITH ... ... 3 ...	71·0	—	—	Mechanical failure on Westward Run
	Group V (Racing Cars)—Class 8 (3,000 c.c. to 5,000 c.c.)				
90	L. McV. WESTON 4½	96·5	—	—	Eastward Run not timed
91	H. J. K. TOWNSHEND 4½	79·4	89·4	84·1	T. D. L. Rose's Team Car
93	W. F. J. BROGDEN 3/4½	94·7	102·4	98·4	1964 = 96·0
	Group V (Racing Cars)—Class 9 (5,000 c.c. to 8,000 c.c.)				
94	G. T. SHOOSMITH 6½	93·1	103·1	97·9	1964 = 90·4
95	B. M. RUSS-TURNER ... ... 4½(S)	108·6	—	—	Mechanical failure on Westward Run
96	H. ROSS ... ... 4½(S)	118·0*	124·3**	121·0	*Best of two Westward Runs by concession **Fastest single Bentley Run 1964 = 86·1
97	E. N. CORNER 8	94·3	105·7	99·7	
	Group V (Racing Cars)—Class 10 (Over 8,000 c.c.)				
98	F. A. SOWDEN 8	123·9	123·8	123·9	Fastest Bentley 1964 = 118·6
OTHER MAKES					
	Group III (Grand Touring Cars) Class 4 (600 c.c. to 700 c.c.)				
57	MISS W. A. ROSS ... ... Hillman Emery Imp ...	77·3*	87·6	83·7	*Best of two Westward Runs by concession
	Group III (Grand Touring Cars) Class 12 (2,500 c.c. to 3,000 c.c.)				
68	G. M. CROZIER ... ... 250 GT Ferrari	133·2	140·6	136·8	
	Group III (Grand Touring Cars) Class 13 (3,000 c.c. to 4,000 c.c.)				
69	T. D. L. ROSS ... ... Aston Martin DB4GT	159·4	167·8	163·5	FASTEST TIME OF DAY
70	E. N. CORNER ... ... Aston Martin DB5 ...	126·6	132·9	129·7	
	Group V (Sports Cars) Class 12 (2,500 c.c. to 3,000 c.c.)				
77	A. R. GOODA ... ... Austin Healey 3000 ...	107·1	118·7	112·6	
	Group IV (Sports Cars) Class 13 (3,000 c.c. to 4,000 c.c.)				
78	R. D. A. WILLS ... ... Lagonda Rapide	73·9	—	—	Mechanical failure on Westward Run
79	J. L. GODDARD ... ... Jaguar D-type	135·6*	140·6	138·1	*Best of two Westward Runs by concession
	Group IV (Sports Cars) Class 14 (4,000 c.c. to 5,000 c.c.)				
84	F. MORLEY ... ... Packard ...	86·8	94·3	90·4	
	Group V (Racing Cars) Class 8 (3,000 c.c. to 5,000 c.c.)				
92	F. A. SOWDEN (Driver—E. Barraclough) Jaguar C-type ...	142·7	146·9	144·7	1964 = 119·1

1965 Antwerp 'Snippets'

The ex Birkin Team Car never really got going and covered most of the distance on only three cylinders. After the first run a badly cracked block was discovered which made it impossible to even consider a return run.

Jack Smith competing for the first time had the misfortune to strip his cross shaft gears alas during his return run.

Stanley Sedgwick in 'Olga' suffered an irritating mishap not on the track but en route out. On arrival at Ostend on the ferry 'Olga' was discovered to have a flat tyre. The crew on board refused to allow the wheel to be changed in situ and insisted on the car being first removed from the ship – petty bureaucratic bloody-mindedness at its worst, resulting in the loss of one perfectly good tyre. Stanley Sedgwick's comments are not recorded – probably just as well.

Appendix Two

SPEED TRIAL RESULTS BY YEAR AT GHENT
Summary of Participating Drivers, their Bentleys, Speeds and Times

SPEED TRIAL RESULTS AT GHENT 1967

Competitors and results were :

		1st run	2nd run	mean k.p.m. =	m.p.h.
A. R. Gooda	S.3 Cont.	190.27	181.27	185.77	115.4
B. M. Russ-Turner	4½(S)	186.63	172.50	179.56	111.6
H. Rose	4½	170.29	162.75	166.62	103.5
F. M. Wilcock	R. Cont.	169.25	160.36	164.80	102.4
B. Dumps	R/S.1	166	154	160	100 *
J. H. Bailey	Mk. 6 4½	158.94	154.18	156.56	97.3
J. R. Nutter	6½	159.01	155.44	157.23	97.7
W. F. J. Brogden	3/4½	129.22	161.22	145.22	90.2
T. D. L. Rose	4½	150.56	136.78	143.67	89.3

It is regretted that the timekeeper was unable to supply more detailed times for this car.

1967 Ghent 'Snippets'
Jack Bailey wrote: "No one had any mechanical trouble except Nutter, who had a puncture, and Bailey whose cigar lighter packed up.

HOW THEY RAN

Name	Type	First Run m.p.h.	Second Run m.p.h.	Average m.p.h.	Remarks
GOODA, R. ...	Bentley S.3	—	—	116·1	2nd Class 13
SHOOSMITH, B. ...	Mk. VI	99·8	100·2	100	4th Class 13
HINE, H.	3 litre	99·8	101·9	100·9	1st Class 11
MORLEY, P. ...	4½ litre	104·8	106·9	105·8	7th Class 12
BATTEN, O. ...	8 litre	112·2	115·8	113·0	4th Class 12
LLEWELLYN, D. ...	3/6½ litre	117·2	120·1	118·9	3rd Class 12
WESTON, I. ...	4½ litre	106·8	109·2	108·2	5th Class 12
ROSE, H.	Mk. VI	107·2	108·3	107·9	6th Class 12
CHESTON, W. R....	4½ litre	85·7	87·7	86·6	8th Class 12
RUSS - TURNER, M.	4½ litre s/c	118·2	120·0	119·1	2nd Class 12
SANDWITH, G. ...	6½ litre	91·1	90·0	90·8	5th Class 13
SHOOSMITH, G. ...	6½ litre	107·8	111·2	109·5	2nd Class 13
MOSS, R. ...	6½ litre	110·8	110·3	110·5	1st Class 13
WILCOCK, M. ...	8 litre	105·6	108·2	107·0	3rd Class 13
GODDARD, J. ...	3/8 litre	88·2	62·2	73·0	6th Class 13 (Fuel starvation)

1968 Ghent 'Snippets'

John Goddard's patrol tank suffered a leak which led to a failure to raise sufficient pressure in the tank to properly feed the carburettors at top revs causing misfiring through fuel starvation and a blow back in the induction which split the hose.

Driver	Car	Speed (m.p.h.)
J. H. Bailey	Lancia Flavia	94·99
D. W. Rumsey	Bentley R.-Cont.	105·82
A. A. Phillips	Jensen 541	104·19
A. R. Gooda	Bentley S.3 Cont.	112·18
R. Gooda	Hillman Imp	100·36
G. Shoosmith	Bentley Speed Six	109·65
B. M. Russ-Turner	Bentley 4½ (S)	116·08
J. R. Nutter	Bentley Speed Six	105·02
Anne Shoosmith	Bentley Mk. VI	103·42
R. Collings	Bentley 4½	96·63
W. Cheston	Bentley 4½	81·76
F. M. Wilcock	Bentley 8	123·79
J. Goddard	Bentley 8 (S)	120·85
F. Sowden	Bentley 8	113·84
G. Shoosmith	Sunbeam G.P.	90·75

Results are the mean of two runs—in opposite directions.

1969 Ghent 'Snippets'

John Goddard's 8 litre broke a piston on the return run, resulting in his turbo charged Bentley merely coasting over the finish line. Just look at his speed and ponder what he might have achieved if all went well.

SPEED TRIAL RESULTS AT GHENT 1970

FLYING KILOMETRE

NAME	MOTOR CAR	SPEED KPH OUT	SPEED KPH IN	AVERAGE KPH	AVERAGE TO NEAREST MPH	POSITION IN CLASS
PROCTOR, J.	MGB.GT	161·218	161·145	161·218	101	2nd Grp. 4, Class 9
SHOOSMITH, B.	LOTUS BRM	176·643	173·913	175·267	110	1st Grp. 4, Class 12
GOODA, A. R.	MASERATI	231·809	235·117	233·463	145+	1st Grp. 6, Class 12
BROWN, D.	JAGUAR XK120	245·398	220·922	233·160	145—	2nd Grp. 6, Class 12
LEATHERS	GILBERN	181·177	175·611	178·394	112	3rd Grp. 6, Class 12
ROSE, H.	BENTLEY S1	172·993	175·843	174·418	110	4th Grp. 6, Class 12
DYMOCK-MAUNSEL, J.	BENTLEY S1	173·829	174·333	174·081	110	5th Grp. 6, Class 12
HARBEN, H.	BENTLEY Sp. 6	161·001	163·907	162·454	102	6th Grp. 6, Class 12
EASTICK, B.	BENTLEY S1	154·506				7th Grp. 6, Class 12 Ret'd mech. trouble
DUMPS, B.	BENTLEY S3	185·950	148·804	185·375	117	1st Grp. 6, Class 13
JONES	BENTLEY S3	175·438	174·081	174·757	110	2nd Grp. 6, Class 13
SHOOSMITH, G.	ROLLS-ROYCE T	146·281	180·813	161·725	101	3rd Grp. 6, Class 13
RUSS-TURNER, B. M.	BENTLEY 4½S	197·585	197·152	197·368	123	1st Grp. Sp. Class 12
WILTON, L. H.	BENTLEY 4½	149·253	150·125	149·688	93	2nd Grp. Sp. Class 12
CHESTON, W.	BENTLEY 4½	134·428	134·178	134·328	84	3rd Grp. Sp. Class 12
COLLINGS	BENTLEY 4½		Times here awaiting ratification			
WILCOCK, F. M.	BENTLEY 8	206·777	213·903	210·280	131	1st Grp. Sp. Class 13
BAILEY, J. H.	BENTLEY 4½	160·786	160·642	160·714	100	2nd Grp. Sp. Class 13
GOODA, R.	BENTLEY 4½	154·972	150·125	152·542	95	3rd Grp. Sp. Class 13
SANDWITH, G.	BENTLEY Sp. 6	146·222	146·639	146·460	91	4th Grp. Sp. Class 13

STANDING START KILOMETRE

NAME	MOTOR CAR	TIME IN SECS. OUT	TIME IN SECS. IN	AVERAGE TIME IN SECS.	POSITION IN CLASS
PROCTOR, J.	MGB GT	35·86	35·47	35·66	2nd Grp. 4, Class 9
SHOOSMITH, B.	LOTUS BRM	32·50	30·88	31·69	1st Grp. 4, Class 12
GOODA, A. R.	MASERATI	28·10	27·76	27·93	2nd Grp. 6, Class 12
BROWN, D.	JAGUAR XK120	26·35	25·82	26·08	1st Grp. 6, Class 12
LEATHERS	GILBERN	29·26	29·39	29·32	3rd Grp. 6, Class 12
ROSE, H.	BENTLEY S1	35·01	34·90	34·94	4th Grp. 6, Class 12
DYMOCK-MAUNSELL, J.	BENTLEY S1	35·34	35·24	35·29	5th Grp. 6, Class 12
HARBEN, H.	BENTLEY Sp. 6	36·26	34·66	35·46	6th Grp. 6, Class 12
EASTICK, B.	BENTLEY S1	37·87	Retired—mechanical trouble		7th Grp. 6, Class 12
DUMPS, B.	BENTLEY S3	32·32	32·06	32·21	1st Grp. 6, Class 13
JONES	BENTLEY S3	33·03	32·92	32·97	2nd Grp. 6, Class 13
SHOOSMITH, G.	ROLLS-ROYCE	33·73	32·47	33·10	3rd Grp. 6, Class 13
RUSS-TURNER, B. M.	BENTLEY 4½	31·99	31·86	31·92	2nd Grp. Sp. Class 12
WILTON, L. H.	BENTLEY 4½	23·42*	38·23	30·82*	1st Grp. Sp. Class 12
COLLINGS, R.	BENTLEY 4½		Times here waiting ratification		
CHESTON, W.	BENTLEY 4½	39·99	39·89	39·94	4th Grp. Sp. Class 12
WILCOCK, F. M.	BENTLEY 8	31·50	29·07	30·28	1st Grp. Sp. Class 13
BAILEY, J. H.	BENTLEY 4½	32·27	32·28	32·27	2nd Grp. Sp. Class 13
GOODA, R.	BENTLEY 4½	34·51	33·93	34·22	3rd Grp. Sp. Class 13
SANDWITH, G.	BENTLEY Sp. 6	37·90	37·08	37·49	4th Grp. Sp. Class 13

*These times are suspect and subject to checking.

1970 Ghent 'Snippets'

Jack Bailey's rather brief article in October's BDC Review of that year does not include any reports of problems.

Confirmed Times for Standing Start and Flying Kilometre—8th May, 1971, Gent, Belgium.

Name	Standing start			Flying kilo		
				Outward	Inward	Aver.
	Outward	Inward	Aver.	m.p.h.	m.p.h.	m.p.h.
Ann Shoosmith, Mk. VI	31.95	31.56	31.75	112	107	109
Bill Thompson, Mk. VI	30.76	30.69	30.72	108	105	106
Adrian Phillips, Maserati	30.56	29.92	30.24	129	122	126
Barry Eastick, Mk. VI	30.13	30.55	30.34	122	122	122
Hugh Harben, R-type	34.31	34.30	34.30	104	101	102
Bob Gooda, Maserati	28.05	27.36	27.70	128	108	117
Rusty Russ-Turner, Single-Seater	32.59	33.91	33.25	123	109	116
Jack Bailey, 4½	30.29	31.20	30.74	101	93	96
Harvey Hine, 4½-litre	37.10	38.43	37.76	83	80	81
Bill Cheston, 4½-litre	39.84	40.49	40.16	84	79	81
Guy Shoosmith, Sunbeam	39.72	39.81	39.76	91	84	87
Len Wilton, 3-litre	42.67	43.66	43.16	77	71	73
David Llewellyn, 3/8-litre	26.27	25.95	26.11	99	93	96
John Goddard, 8-litre	31.38	33.91	32.64	129	123	126
Michael Wilcock, 8-litre	29.73	30.62	30.17	119	125	123
Peter Morley, Napier	29.53	—	—	105	—	—
Patricia Gooda S.3	32.04	32.17	32.10	114	115	115

1971 Ghent 'Snippets'

John Goddard again had problems; but clutch slip and a hole in No 5 piston did not prevent him from making fastest kilometre time of all the Bentleys.

Jack Bailey's front wing flew off and appeared to overtake him at great speed but the BDC Review reported: "compared to other Bailey blow ups this was a mere trifle!"

David Llewellyn himself writes about his performance at Ghent in 1971: "In my 3/8 Bentley, I mistook one of the marker posts. But my real problem was fuel starvation. Competing in sprints and races in the U.K. one could measure in seconds the time one had the throttle open in top gear. In Ghent it was minutes, so when I got fuel starvation I quickly backed off before I burnt a hole in a piston. Hence my times for the Flying Kilometre were dreadful.

The President of the Belgian Club bought himself a new Ferrari Daytona for the event. The Review records that I had the fastest Bentley time for the Standing Start Kilometre. It does not record, that to the embarrassment of the Club President, my banger also beat his new Ferrari! I achieved FTD on the Standing Start kilometre!

The speed of the car has subsequently been timed at 135 mph. With a higher back axle ratio this could have been noticeably improved."

Competitor	Car	m.p.h.	
B. M. Russ-Turner	4½ S/C Birkin	125	
H. N. Harben	4½ Hybrid	94	
G. Russell	4½	93	Mean
H. Morten	4½	Retd.	speed
D. Grew	3	76	of two
J. Goddard	3/8 T/C	158	runs in
F. M. Wilcock	8	132	opposite
B. Eastick	4.9 S1 Special	126	directions.
J. Proctor	4.9 S1 Continental	108	
R. Palmer	4.9 S1 Special	97	

1972 Ghent 'Snippets'

Hugh Harben couldn't start his 4½, when about to leave the garage. As the Review reported: "Own up who left a matchstick separating the ignition points on the Presidential motor before you are expelled from the Club!"

Hamish Morten melted two pistons in his 4½ which as the BDC Review charmingly understated: "spoilt his run".

Wilcocks 8 litre departed Ghent on return on 5 cylinders, indicating earlier failure on his run but this didn't affect the Bentley sufficiently to prevent it achieving a mean average speed on 127 mph.

John Goddard at last enjoyed trouble free runs and achieved the incredible record speed of 158.2 mph for the flying kilometre.

FLYING KILO.

Competitor	Car	* m.p.h.
Wilcock, Frederick	Jaguar V.12 E Coupe	143.85
Dymock-Maunsell, John	Jaguar E C.12	140.07
Gooda, Bob	Maserati Bora C	158.42
Filbee, John	Jaguar E Type	141.13
Nutter, John	Bentley Speed 6	96.92
Russell, Gordon J.	Bentley 4½	86.37
Woodrow-Hill, Graham	Bentley 3	80.52
Hine, Harvey P.	Morris Cowley	49.70
Eastick, Barrington	Bentley VI/S.1 Cont.	131.66
Russ-Turner, B. M.	Bentley Convertible	114.54
Palmer, Ronald	Bentley Mk. VI	100.08
Willson, Anthony	Bentley Mk. VI/S.1	96.71

* Mean speed of two runs.

STANDING KILO.

Competitor	Car	* m.p.h.	† secs.
Wilcock, Frederick	Jaguar V.12 E Coupe	84.89	26.35
Dymock-Maunsell, John	Jaguar E V.12	80.49	27.79
Filbee, John	Jaguar E Type	83.69	N.R.
Gooda, Bob	Maserati Bora C	83.25	26.87
Nutter, John	Bentley Speed 6	70.99	31.51
Russell, Gordon	Bentley 4½	57.61	38.83
Woodrow-Hill, Graham	Bentley 3	53.62	41.72
Hine, Harvey P.	Morris Cowley	39.06	57.27
Eastick, Barrington	Bentley VI/S.1 Cont.	73.85	30.29
Willson, Anthony	Bentley Mk. VI/S.1	69.17	32.34
Palmer, Ronald	Bentley Mk. VI	67.72	33.03
Russ-Turner, B. M.	Bentley Convertible	67.16	33.30

* Mean speed—two runs.   † Mean time—two runs.

1973 Ghent entitled "the Battle of Crewe" in Bill Cheston's Report in the BDC Review.

Barry Eastick took the honours as fastest of Crewe's 4 entries at 131.66 mph – indeed his was the fastest of all Bentleys competing that year.

Ann Shoosmith suffered valve seat coming adrift, the turbocharger had blown a rubber hose and the consequent weakness had burned the top off a piston.

John Nutter had some magneto trouble which the results show reduced his average.

<u>Harvey Hine</u> according to Bill Cheston caused the sensation of the day: "The crowd could barely conceal its curiosity as to what was now coming down the track; which car had such an incredibly weak and alarmingly wobbly head light (only one lit) but still for all apparent agitation took so long to arrive. Fred Hoffman used his glasses, strained his eyes, and then after about 10 minutes announced "Gentlemen, it's the Bull Nose Morris". Harvey Hine motoring past with nonchalance, a royal wave to the plebs, elbow resting elegantly on the side, dicky firmly locked against the hazards of air stream, hood stowed neatly, radiator polished. This lovely car recorded an average speed of 50 mph which if you know your Bull Nose Morris is pretty fast. It was however the only car present to record a standing kilo at a speed that was less than the number of seconds to achieve it!"

Harvey Hine in 2010 relates: "The organizers insisted on my running in the Flying Kilometre, a ridiculous thing to do. Anyway I said: "well alright then". I went and did it and averaged 49 miles an hour which I was delighted about. Very good! I was chuffed about that. Anyway they invented a class for me and in the prize giving in the evening I was awarded first prize and also second prize!"

ROYAL AUTOMOBILE CLUB DES FLANDRES
8è KILOMETRE LANCE INTERNATIONAL DE GAND
4 mai 1974

		Out	Back	Average	Speed Km./hr.
Harvey Hine	Standing	30,75	—	—	117.073
	Flying	—	—	—	—
Cyril Wadsworth ...	Standing	38,93	40,10	39,51	91.116
	Flying	25,58	26,89	26,23	137.247
Len Wilton	Standing	36,27	36,58	36,42	98.846
	Flying	24,76	24,84	24,80	145.454
Ronald Palmer ...	Standing	31,33	31,75	31,54	114.140
	Flying	21,29	22,32	21,80	165.137
Graham Woodrow-Hill	Standing	42,44	43,93	43,18	83.371
	Flying	26,58	29,53	28,05	128.342
Gordon Russell ...	Standing	53,48	40,53	47,00	76.595
	Flying	24,65	26,86	25,75	139.805
Peter Morley	Standing	26,05	25,23	25,64	140.405
	Flying	18,67	19,10	18,88	190.677
James Howarth ...	Standing	39,21	40,76	39,98	90.045
	Flying	26,83	27,88	27,35	131.627
" Rusty " Russ-Turner	Standing	28,77	—	—	125.130
	Flying	19,62	—	—	183.486

1974 Ghent 'Snippets'

'Rusty' Russ Turner in his 4½ Blower had a failed piston as a result of 4,500 revs!

Harvey Hine in his 4½ with a new engine had trouble with his water pump which packed up and caused it to boil.

Gordon Russell in spite of running on only one mag achieved over 139 mph.

RESULTS

Vintage

1st	Bob May	6½-litre	161.218 k.p.h.	100.761 m.p.h.
2nd	Harvey Hine	4½-litre	158.940 k.p.h.	99.300 m.p.h.
3rd	Rusty Russ-Turner	4½(S)	142.970 k.p.h.	89.356 m.p.h.
4th	Don Balmer	3-litre	124.352 k.p.h.	77.720 m.p.h.
5th	David Helman	3-litre	123.451 k.p.h.	77.157 m.p.h.
6th	David Rolfe	4½-litre	94.562 k.p.h.	59.101 m.p.h.

Post-Vintage

1st	Brian Shoosmith	Mk. VI/S.1 Cont.	204.778 k.p.h.	127.986 m.p.h.
2nd	Ron Palmer	Mk. VI/S.1	172.827 k.p.h.	108.017 m.p.h.
3rd	Len Wilton	3-litre/S.1	152.671 k.p.h.	95.419 m.p.h.

1975 Ghent 'Snippets'

John Nutter had No 6 piston collapse on his outward run on the 8 litre engined Speed 6.

'Rusty' Russ Turner yet again had a problem – this time an exhaust valve being stuck open.

David Rolfe competing for the first time, suffered misfiring affecting his speed.

10th STANDING/FLYING KILOMETRE, GHENT, BELGIUM
OFFICIAL RESULTS OF BENTLEYS

No.	Name	Model	Km.	Out m.p.h.	Return m.p.h.	Average m.p.h.	Expected m.p.h.
69	RUSS-TURNER, Rusty	The Birkin	Standing Flying	71.338 127.190	75.722 127.190	72.023 127.190	120
71	GAUNTLETT, Victor	4½	Standing Flying	65.522 103.971	65.192 101.580	65.350 102.740	100
72	GAUNTLETT, Victor	4½	Standing Flying	71.384 93.633	— —	— —	
73	GAUNTLETT, Jean	Corniche	Standing Flying	71.839 117.863	72.139 117.310	71.977 117.555	105
75	SHOOSMITH, Ann	4½ Team Car	Standing Flying	63.274 101.810	63.812 98.125	63.542 99.911	92
76	WILCOCK, Michael	8	Standing Flying	74.850 112.332	74.825 133.057	74.825 121.819	110
77	GAUNTLETT, Victor	Corniche	Standing Flying	71.338 116.279	72.628 119.048	71.977 117.617	115
79	TRENTHAM, Martin	R-Type Spec.	Standing Flying	71.090 111.442	74.950 117.678	72.957 114.445	100
81	BALMER, Don	3	Standing Flying	49.084 72.792	48.744 69.660	48.913 71.180	63
82	PARKINSON, Barry	4½	Standing Flying	59.273 95.623	59.055 95.017	59.164 95.299	96
83	TEALL, Charles	Mk. VI Spec.	Standing Flying	64.489 91.650	64.767 90.507	64.618 91.057	101
84	MAY, Bob	Speed Six	Standing Flying	56.533 59.273	57.064 102.459	56.790 75.100	101
85	GUPPY, John	Mk. VI Spec.	Standing Flying	75.251 97.869	76.976 100.897	76.091 99.338	125
86	GODDARD, J. (Driver J. Guppy)	8 turbo/c.	Standing Flying	82.630 139.405	85.227 132.900	83.893 136.034	140

1976 Ghent 'Snippets'

Victor Gauntlett in Russ Turner's ex 4¼ only made the outward run successfully, being towed back with pistons Nos 2 & 3 hors de combat. This alas prevented his wife, Jean, and Ian MacLaren who were to have used this car, from having a go in it.

Appendix Three

FASTEST BENTLEY PERFORMANCE EACH YEAR
Mean Average of Two Runs over Flying Kilometre

	Year	Driver	Bentley Model	mph
ANTWERP	1959	Forrest Lycett	8 litre	140.35
	1962	Forrest Lycett	8 litre	141.13
	1963	Frank Sowden	8 litre	42.54 secs (mph not recorded in reports)
	1964	Frank Sowden	8 litre	118.61
	1965	Frank Sowden	8 litre	123.9
GHENT	1967	Bob Gooda	S3 Continental	115.4
	1968	Rusty Russ Turner	4½ litre supercharged	119.1
	1969	Michael Wilcock	8 litre	123.79
	1970	Michael Wilcock	8 litre	131 to nearest mph
	1971	John Goddard	8 litre	126 to nearest mph
	1972	John Goddard	8 litre turbocharged	158.2
	1973	Barry Eastick	Mk VI/S1 Continental	136.66
	1974	Peter Morley	Napier Bentley	190.68 kph = 119.175 mph
	1975	Brian Shoosmith	Mk VI/S1 Continental	127.99
	1976	John Guppy	8 litre turbocharged (John Goddard's car)	136.03

Appendix Four

DRIVERS ACHIEVING OVER 100 MILES PER HOUR IN BENTLEYS AT ANTWERP

Listed in order of highest speed and year achieved. Speeds shown are mean average mph for both runs unless, where in brackets, were only achieved on a single run one way.

Speed	Driver	Bentley Model	Comments	Year of Trial
141.131	Lycett F	8 litre		1962
140.845	Lycett F	8 litre		1959
136.149	Goddard J	3/8		1962
127.897	Sedgwick S	6½		1962
127.818	Sedgwick S	6½		1959
127.818	Burton GHG	6½		1959
125.599	Sears J	4½ SC		1962
125.304	Sears J	4½ SC		1959
123.9	Sowden FA	8 litre		1965
123.414	Batten O	8 litre		1959
121.374	Batten O	8 litre		1962
121.0	Rose H	4½ SC		1965
119.008	Pounds HS	4½		1959
118.607	Sowden FA	8 litre		1964
116.265	Burton GHG	3/4½		1962
114.4	Gooda AR	S3 Continental		1965
114.246	Gooda AR	S3 Continental		1964
114.012	Pounds HS	4½		1962
109.760	Sedgewick S	R Continental		1962

Continued overleaf

Speed	Driver	Bentley Model	Comments	Year of Trial
109.385	Rose H	4½		1962
109.289	Rose H	4½		1959
(108.6	Russ Turner BM	4½ SC	One way only above 100 mph	1965)
108.012	Pounds HS	4½		1964
107.390	Burton GHG	3/5.6 litre		1964
(108.8	Silcock DG	R Continental 4.6 litres	One way only over 100 mph	1965)
105.765	Morley FP	8 litre		1964
(105.7	Corner N	8 litre	Over 100 mph only one way	1965)
104.334	Russ Turner BM	Mk VI (S)		1964
104.110	Rose L	R Continental		1964
(103.466	Morley FP	4½	Over 100 mph only one way	1964)
(103.370	Shoosmith G	6½	Over 100 mph only one way	1964)
(103.1	Shoosmith G	6½	Over 100 mph only one way	1965)
102.424	Sedgwick S	R Continental		1964
(102.4	Brogden WFJ	3/4½	Over 100 mph only one way	1965)
101.9	Sedgwick S	R Continental (4.9)		1965
(100.221	Sedgwick S	R Continental	Over 100 mph only one way	1964)
(100.027	Llewellyn D	3 litre	Over 100 mph only one way	1959)

Appendix Four

DRIVERS ACHIEVING OVER 100 MILES PER HOUR IN BENTLEYS AT GHENT

Listed in order of highest speed achieved for mean average of 2 completed runs.

Speed	Driver	Bentley Model	Comments	Year of Trial
158.2	Goddard J	3/8 Turbocharged		1972
136.034	Guppy J	3/8 Turbocharged	Driving Goddard's car	1976
132	Wilcock FM	8 litre		1972
131	Wilcock FM	8 litre		1970
131.66	Eastick B	Mk VI/S1 Continental		1973
127.986	Shoosmith B	Mk VIS1 Continental		1975
126	Goddard J	8 litre		1971
126	Eastick B	S1 Special 4.9 litre		1972
125	Russ Turner BM	ex Birkin 4½ litre SC		1972
123.79	Wilcock FM	8 litre		1969
123	Wilcock FM	8 litre		1971
123	Russ Turner BM	4½ SC		1970
122	Eastick B	Mk VI		1971
121.819	Wilcock FM	8 litre		1976
120.85	Goddard J	3/8 Turbocharged		1969
119.173	Morley P	Napier Bentley		1974
119.1	Russ Turner BM	4½ SC		1968
118.9	Llewellyn D	3/6½		1968
117.617	Gauntlett V	Corniche		1976

Continued overleaf

Speed	Driver	Bentley Model	Comments	Year of Trial
117.555	Gauntlett J	Corniche		1976
117	Dumps B	S3		1970
116.1	Gooda AR	S3		1968
116.08	Russ Turner BM	4½ S ex Birkin		1969
116	Russ Turner BM	4½ S ex Birkin		1971
115.4	Gooda AR	S3 Continental		1967
115	Gooda Patricia	S3		1971
114.678	Russ Turner BM	4½ SC		1974
114.54	Russ Turner BM	Continental		1973
114.445	Trentham M	R Type Special		1976
113.84	Sowden F	8 litre		1969
113	Batten O	8 litre		1968
112.18	Gooda AR	S3 Continental		1969
111.6	Russ Turner BM	4½ SC		1967
110.5	Moss R	6½		1968
110	Jones	S3		1970
110	Rose H	S1		1970
110	Dymock Maunsell J	S1		1970
109.65	Shoosmith G	Speed Six		1969
109.5	Shoosmith G	Speed Six		1968
109.2	Weston I	4½		1968
109	Shoosmith A			1971
108.2	Weston I	4½		1968
108.017	Palmer R	Mk VI/S1		1975
108	Proctor J	S1 Continental 4.9 litre		1972
107.96	Rose H	4½		1968
107	Wilcock M	8 litre		1968

Speed	Driver	Bentley Model	Comments	Year of Trial
106	Thompson W	Mk VI		1971
105.82	Rumsey DW	R Continental		1969
105.8	Morley P	Napier Bentley		1971
105.02	Nutter JR	Speed Six		1969
103.5	Rose H	4½		1967
103.42	Shoosmith A	Mk VI		1969
103.27	Palmer R	Mk VI		1974
102.74	Gauntlett V	4½		1976
102.4	Wilcock M	R Continental		1967
102	Harben H	R Type		1971
102	Harben H	Speed Six		1970
100.8	Palmer R	Mk VI		1973
100.761	May Bob	Speed Six		1973
100	Shoosmith B	Mk VI		1968
100	Dumps B	R/S1		1967
100	Bailey J	4¼		1970

Appendix Four

DRIVERS OF BENTLEYS ACHIEVING OVER 100 MILES PER HOUR
IN A RUN AT GHENT

But <u>only in one</u> direction – not completing both runs at over 100 mph. Listed in speed order.

Speed	Driver	Bentley Model	Year of Trial
113.8	Batten O	8 litre	1968
112	Shoosmith A	Mk VI	1971
111.2	Shoosmith G	6½	1968
102.459	May Bob	Speed Six	1976
101.810	Shoosmith A	4½	1976
101	Bailey J	4¼	1971
100.897	Guppy J	Mk VI Special	1976

Appendix Five

DRIVERS WHO COMPETED IN A BENTLEY IN THE TRIALS
AT ANTWERP and/or GHENT

Listed alphabetically, together with the year(s) of their participation.

Bailey Jack	65, 67, 70, 71
Balmer Don	75, 76
Batten Oliver	59, 62, 63, 68
Brogden John	62, 63, 64, 65, 67
Burton George	62, 63, 64
Cheston Bill	68, 69, 70, 71
Collings Roger	69, 70
Corner Neil	65
Dumps B	67, 70
Dymock Maunsell John	70
Eastick Barry	70, 71, 72, 73
Gauntlett Victor	76
Gauntlett Jean	76
Glydon Rupert	64
Goddard John	62, 68, 69, 71, 72
Gooda Bob	64, 65, 67, 68, 69, 70
Gooda Patricia	71
Grew Douglas	72
Guppy John	76
Harben Hugh	70, 71, 72
Helman David	75
Hine Harvey	64, 68, 71, 74, 75
Howarth James	74
Jones	70
Llewellyn David	59, 62, 68, 71
Lycett Forrest	59, 62
May Bob	75, 76
Morley Charles	63
Morley Peter	64, 68, 71, 74
Morten Hamish	62, 63, 72

Continued overleaf

Moss Dick	68
Nutter John	65, 67, 69, 73
Palmer Ron	72,73,74,75
Parkinson Barry	76
Pounds Harold	59, 62, 64
Proctor John	72
Rolfe David	75
Rose Harry	59, 62, 63, 64, 65, 67, 68, 70
Rose L	64
Rose Miss WA	64
Rose TDL	67
Rumsey DW	69
Russell Gordon	72, 73, 74
Russell Vick	64
Russ Turner Rusty	63, 64, 65, 67, 68, 69, 70, 71, 72, 73, 74, 75, 76
Sandwith Geoffrey	65, 68, 70
Sears Jack	59, 62
Sedgwick Stanley	59, 62, 63, 64, 65
Shoosmith Ann	69, 71, 76
Shoosmith Brian	68, 75
Shoosmith Guy	64, 65, 68, 69
Silcock DG	65
Smith Jack	65
Sowden Frank	63, 64, 65, 69
Teal Charles	76
Thompson Bill	71
Townshend Tony	65
Trentham Martin	76
Wadsworth Cyril	74
Weston I McV	63, 65, 68
Wilcock Mike	67, 68, 69, 70, 71, 72, 76
Williamson	62
Wilson Tony	73
Wilton Len	70, 71, 74, 75
Woodhead Garry	64
Woodrow-Hill Graham	73, 74

Belgian Recollections

Perhaps some of the final words should come from a Belgian who witnessed these events as a teenager. Rene Molle writes in 2010:

"Dear Mr Bodfish

The Good Old Days of the speed trials at Ghent

The teenagers like me were thrilled by the idea of admiring racing cars at speed on a public road without any fence nor controller around the pits. Many roads were empty on the Sundays, open access was easy, the spectators were not numerous. The roads were new stretches of unfinished dual carriage ways, straight and perfectly horizontal. The city councils were kind to license such events. They provided policemen and road signs.

We reached the climax the weekends when a club arrived from UK, joyful entrants in green dinosaurs noisy and terrifically fast. A few Belgians paid attention. Our English was not fluent, fifty percent from the US forces of 1945 and a little less from the American movies. Following that American influence we imagined the dream cars like the ones advertised in Collier's and in The Sunday Evening Post: greenhouses with a bonnet the size of the deck of an airplane carrier, two colours of ice cream. That developed 25 years of disdain for the "old cars" before we became aware the survivors of the war were collector's items. The chaps were welcomed by a small party of enthusiasts. They were typically British: ageless suit, soft voice, polite company and fondness for Belgian beer and French wine.

Such a love for useless old bangers surprised but the meetings were so much enjoyed that long after they were remembered at our Belgian Veteran Car Club. Today I can't see the border between the real facts and the fake anecdotes of that glorious motoring. We were told that a party sailed from Australia, cars and crews in a small passenger-cargo ship. Some were back to see again the countries of the war. Most among them were involved to make the journey the adventure of a lifetime. A sailor said: the wake was not followed by the porpoises, only by the empty bottles. I found that was the first infectious contact of my incurable auto-mania. It was a remote project for me, a stimulus, and 20 years later I was able to buy a 4½ litre in 1972 and joined the BDC.

With best regards

Rene MOLLE, JODOIGNE, Belgium."

Tailpiece

From Bentley Drivers Club Review of 1975

There was a young man of Ghent

Who drove very fast in a Bent

But heedless of trouble

His pace he did double

And instead of coming he went

- Traditional